Ghost Hunter's Guide
to
New Orleans

For you
10th Anniversary
return trip —

♡

Ghost Hunter's Guide
to
New Orleans

By Jeff Dwyer

PELICAN PUBLISHING COMPANY
Gretna 2007

The word "Pelican" and the depiction of a pelican are trademarks
of Pelican Publishing Company, Inc., and are registered in the
U.S. Patent and Trademark Office.

Library of Congress Cataloging-in-Publication Data

Dwyer, Jeff.
    Ghost hunter's guide to New Orleans / by Jeff Dwyer.
        p. cm.
    Includes index.
    ISBN-13: 978-1-58980-408-1 (pbk. : alk. paper)
    1. Ghosts—Louisiana—New Orleans. 2. Haunted places—
Louisiana—New Orleans. I. Title.
    BF1472.U6D868 2007
    133.109763'35—dc22

                                                    2007013325

Printed in the United States of America
Published by Pelican Publishing Company, Inc.
1000 Burmaster Street, Gretna, Louisiana 70053

To my mother,
Marjorie L. Dwyer,
who always believed in me and in ghosts

Contents

Acknowledgments

Special thanks to my literary agent, Sue Janet Clark, for invaluable guidance and endless patience; to my friends at Pelican Publishing, especially Amy Kirk, John Scheyd, and Nina Kooij, for making my association with the company a great pleasure; and to my wife, Darlene Dwyer, for unfailing encouragement and support.

Introduction

Who believes in ghosts? People from every religion, culture, and gen-eration believe that ghosts exist. The popularity of ghosts and haunted places in books, televisions programs, and movies reflects a belief held by many people that other dimensions and spiritual entities exist.

In 2000, a Gallup poll discovered a significant increase in the number of Americans who believe in ghosts since the question was first asked in 1978. Thirty-one percent of respondents said they believed ghosts existed. In 1978, only 11 percent admitted to believ-ing in ghosts. Less than a year later, Gallup found that 42 percent of the public believed a house could be haunted but only 28 percent believed that we can hear from or mentally communicate with some-one who has died. A 2003 Harris poll found an astounding 51 per-cent of Americans believed in ghosts. As with preceding polls, belief in ghosts was greatest among females. More young people accepted the idea of ghosts than older people. Forty-four percent of people age 18 to 29 admitted a belief in ghosts compared with 13 percent of those older than 65.

In October 2001, Home and Garden TV conducted a survey on its Web site. When asked, "Do you believe in ghosts?" 87 percent of respondents said "Yes!" Fifty-one percent indicated they had seen a ghost, but only 38 percent would enter a haunted house alone at night. There is no way of knowing how many people have seen or heard a ghost only to feel too embarrassed, foolish, or frightened to admit it. Many ghost hunters and spiritual investigators believe a vast majority of people have seen or heard something from the other world, but failed to recognize it.

A number of broadcast networks have recognized the phenomenal interest in paranormal phenomena. In the summer of 2004, the Sci Fi channel launched a weekly one-hour primetime program on ghost hunting. Sci Fi also airs programs that investigate psychic abilities, reincarnation, telekinesis, and many other fascinating topics. NBC broadcasts a weekly primetime drama that follows the true-life experiences of a medium who communicates with ghosts in order to solve crimes, and CBS joined the trend by offering another fact-based drama called *Ghost Whisperer*. In addition, more than 2,000,000 references to ghosts, ghost hunting, haunted places, or related paranormal phenomena can be found on the Internet. Clearly, interest in these areas is widespread.

The recent worldwide interest in ghosts is not a spin-off of the New Age movement or the current popularity of angels or the manifestation of some new religious process. The suspicion or recognition that ghosts exist is simply the reemergence of one of mankind's oldest and most basic beliefs—there is a life after death.

Ancient writings from many cultures describe apparitions and a variety of spirit manifestations that include tolling bells, chimes, disembodied crying or moaning, and whispered messages. Legends and ancient books include descriptions of ghosts, dwelling places of spirits, and periods of intense spiritual activity related to seasons or community events such as festivals or crop harvests. Vital interactions between the living and deceased have been described. Many ancient cultures included dead people or their spirits in community life. Spirits of the dead were sought as a source of guidance, wisdom, and protection for the living. Many believers of the world's oldest religions agree that non-living entities may be contacted for guidance or may be seen on the earthly plane. Among these are visions of saints, the Virgin Mary, and angels.

Ancient sites of intense spiritual activity in Arizona, New Mexico, and Central and South America are popular destinations for travelers seeking psychic or spiritual experiences. More modern local sites, where a variety of paranormal events have occurred, are also popular destinations for adventurous living souls. Amateur and professional ghost hunters seek the spirits of the dearly departed in New Orleans' historic sites, antebellum mansions, old restaurants, and countless other places around south Louisiana, including graveyards and homes. Modern buildings, parks, theaters, and ships, such as the USS *Kidd* in Baton Rouge, also serve as targets for ghost hunters.

Throughout the past two millennia, the popularity of the belief in ghosts has waxed and waned, similar to religious activity. When a rediscovery of ghosts and their roles in our lives occurs, skeptics label the notion a fad or an aberration of modern lifestyles. Perhaps people are uncomfortable with the idea that ghosts exist because it involves an examination of our nature and our concepts of life, death, and afterlife. These concepts are most often considered in the context of religion, yet ghost hunters recognize that acceptance of the reality of ghosts, and a life after death, is a personal decision, having nothing to do with religious beliefs or church doctrine. An intellectual approach enables the ghost hunter to explore haunted places without religious bias or fears.

The greater frequency of ghost manifestations in the New Orleans area, as evidenced by documentary reports on TV and other news media, reflects some people's open-mindedness and wide-spread interest in ghostly experiences. Judging by the incredible popularity of New Orleans ghost tours and history tours of plantation mansions, a lot of visitors believe in the possibility that ghostly phenomena can be experienced here. Ghost hunting is becoming a weekend pastime for many adventurous souls. Advertisement of haunted inns, restaurants, and historical sites is commonplace. It is always fun, often very exciting, and may take ghost hunters places they never dreamed of going.

ABOUT THIS BOOK

Chapter 1 of this book will help you, the ghost hunter, to research and organize your own ghost hunt. Chapters 2 through 5 describe several locations at which ghostly activity has been reported. Unlike other collections of ghost stories and descriptions of haunted places, this book emphasizes access. Addresses of each haunted site are included along with other information to assist you in locating and entering the location. Several appendices offer organizational material for your ghost hunts, including a Sighting Report Form to document your adventures, lists of suggested reading and videos, Internet resources, and organizations you may contact about your experiences with ghosts.

GHOST HUNTING IN NEW ORLEANS AND SOUTH LOUISIANA

For some people, the very word "ghost" immediately brings to mind visions of ancient European castles, foggy moors, and dark, wind-swept ramparts where brave knights battled enemies of the crown or heroines threw themselves to their deaths. The fact is that ghosts are everywhere. A history based in antiquity that includes dark dungeons, hidden catacombs, or ancient ruins covered with a veil of sorrow and pain is not essential, but contemporary versions of these elements are quite common in many American cities.

Indeed, New Orleans, and nearby communities, have all the ingredients necessary for successful ghost hunting. The region has been populated for nearly 300 years with people from a variety of cultures who experienced tremendous changes in their lives. These include the transition from a French colony to a Spanish possession in 1762, return to French rule in 1800, the Louisiana Purchase by the U.S. in 1803, military campaigns including the War of 1812 and the Civil War, the yellow fever epidemics of the 1840s and '50s, fires that destroyed large portions of the city in 1788 and 1794, and other disasters such as hurricanes and floods.

The widespread devastation caused by Hurricane Katrina on August 29, 2005, added more spirits to the Crescent City's ghost legacy and powerful emotions that left haunting imprints on the town and neighboring communities. After the hurricane struck, rescue workers reported lights in buildings that had no electricity. While they conducted their searches, footsteps and moving doors were reportedly heard in buildings found to be deserted.

Throughout the region's history there have been countless opportunities for the spirits of the dearly departed to feel a need to stay on. There are many old hotels and restaurants, plantation mansions, slave quarters, neighborhoods, forts, barrooms, churches, and ships inhabited by ghosts who are often seen or sensed. The lost souls are often the result of violent or unexpected death, often at an early age. These unfortunate people passed with great emotional anguish, leaving their souls with a desire to achieve their life's objectives, or with a sense of obligation to offer protection to a particular place or person. Some ghosts remain on the earthly plane to provide guidance for someone still alive or for revenge.

New Orleans has had its share of criminal activities and social injustice. This has produced many disadvantaged, used, abused, and forlorn people who remain with us after their death. Their souls seek lost dreams while they remain attached to what little they gained during their difficult lives. Many ghosts, harboring resentment, pain, a sense of loss, or a desire to complete their unfinished business, still roam the darkened halls of aging mansions, hotels, theaters, cemeteries, modern buildings, and many other places throughout the region that are accessible to the public.

WHAT IS A GHOST?

A ghost is some aspect of the personality, spirit, consciousness, energy, mind, or soul that remains after the body dies. When any of these are detected by the living—through sight, sound, odor, or movement—the manifestation is called an apparition by parapsychologists. The rest of us call it a ghost. How the ghost manifests itself is unknown. There seems to be a close association, however, between aspects of the entity's life and its manifestation as a ghost. These include a sudden, traumatic death, strong ties to loved ones who survived the entity or a particular place, unfinished business, strong emotions such as hatred and anger, or a desire for revenge.

Ghosts differ from other paranormal phenomena by their display of intelligent action. This includes interaction with the living, performance of a purposeful activity, or a response to ongoing changes in the environment. Ghosts may speak to the living, warning of a foreseen accident or disaster, giving advice, or expressing their love, anger, remorse, or disappointment. They may try to complete some project or duty they failed to finish before death. Some ghosts try to move furniture, room decorations, and the like to suit their preferences.

Some ghosts appear solid and function as living beings because they are unaware they are dead. Others appear as partial apparitions because they are confused about the transition from life to death. Occasionally, paranormal activity is bizarre, frightening, or dangerous to witnesses. Objects may fly about, strange sounds may be heard, or accidents happen. This kind of activity is attributed to a poltergeist or noisy ghost. Most authorities believe that living people, not the dead, cause these manifestations. Generally, someone under great emotional stress releases psychic energy that creates subtle or spectacular changes in the environment.

Noises commonly associated with a poltergeist include tapping on walls or ceilings, heavy footsteps, shattered glass, the ringing of telephones, and running water. Objects may move about on tables or floors or fly across a room. Furniture may spin or tip over. Dangerous objects such as knives, hammers, or pens may hit people. These poltergeist events may last only a few days to a year or more. Discovery and removal of the emotionally unstable, living agent often terminates them.

HAUNTINGS

Hauntings and apparitions may not be the same thing. In fact, some professional ghost hunters and parapsychologists make a clear distinction between these two kinds of paranormal phenomena. They share a lot of the same features in terms of what witnesses see, feel, or smell, but a haunting may occur without the presence of a spiritual entity or consciousness of a dead person. People have reported seeing the pale, transparent images of the deceased walking in hallways, climbing stairs, or sitting in rocking chairs or in seats on airplanes, trains, buses, or restaurants. Some have been seen sleeping in beds, hanging by a rope from a tree, or walking through walls. Most commonly, a partial apparition is seen, but witnesses have reported seeing entire armies engaged in battle. Unlike ghosts, hauntings do not display intelligent action with respect to the location—they don't manipulate your new computer—and they do not interact with the living.

Hauntings may be environmental imprints, recordings of something that happened at a location as a result of the repetition of intense emotion. As such, they tend to be associated with a specific place or object, not a particular person. The ghostly figures tend to perform some kind of task or activity that is repetitive. Sometimes the haunting is so repetitive that witnesses feel as though they are watching a video loop that plays the same brief scene over and over. A good example is the image of a deceased grandmother who makes appearances seated in her favorite rocking chair. Another example is Pere Dagobert, priest of New Orleans' St. Louis Cathedral from 1745 to 1776. His apparition is often seen walking Pirate's Alley next to the church. His melodic, tenor voice is heard, singing a traditional Catholic burial hymn.

There is a lot of evidence that people can trigger and experience these environmental recordings by visiting the particular site, touching an object that was a key element of the event, and psychically connecting with the event. Images of hauntings have been picked up on still and video film and digital recordings. The location of strong environmental imprints can also be discovered through devices such as electromagnetic field detectors. Higher magnetic readings have been found at locations where psychics frequently experience hauntings.

HOW DOES A GHOST MANIFEST ITSELF?

Ghosts interact with our environment in a variety of ways that may have something to do with the strength of their personality, level of confusion concerning their transformation by death, talents or skills they possessed in life, personal objectives, or level of frustration in getting our attention. Some ghosts create odors or sounds, particularly those associated with their habits, such as cigar smoke or whistling. The odors of tobacco, oranges, and old rope are most commonly reported. Sounds, including voice messages, may be detected with an audio recorder (see Electronic Voice Phenomenon). Ghost hunters have recorded greetings, warnings, screams, sobbing, and expressions of love.

One of the most common ghostly activities is moving objects. Ghosts like to knock over stacks of cards or coins, turn doorknobs, scatter matchsticks, and move keys. For many, it appears easy to manipulate light switches and TV remotes, move windows or doors, or push chairs around. Some ghosts have the power to throw objects, pull pictures from a wall, or move heavy items. As a rule, ghosts cannot tolerate disturbances within the place they haunt. If you tilt a wall-mounted picture, the ghost will set it straight. Obstacles placed in the ghost's path may be pushed aside.

These seemingly minor indications of ghostly activity should be recorded for future reference on the Sighting Report Form in Appendix A.

Ghosts can also create changes in the physical qualities of an environment. Ice cold breezes and unexplained gusts of wind are often the first signs that a ghost is present. Moving or stationary cold spots, with temperatures several degrees below surrounding areas, have been detected with reliable instruments. Temperature changes sometimes occur with a feeling that the atmosphere has thickened, as if the room was suddenly filled with unseen people.

Devices that detect changes in magnetic, electrical, or radio fields have been used in the search for ghosts. However, detected changes may be subject to error, interference by other electrical devices, or misinterpretation. Measurements indicating the presence of a ghost may be difficult to capture on a permanent record.

Ghosts may create images on still cameras (film or digital) and video recorders, such as luminous fogs, balls of light called orbs, streaks of light, or the partial outline of body parts. In the 1860s, this was called "spirit photography." Modern digital photographs are easily edited and make it difficult to produce convincing proof of ghostly activity.

Humanoid images are the prized objective of most ghost hunters but they are the rarest to be experienced. When such images occur, they are often partial, revealing only a head and torso with an arm or two. The feet are seldom seen, and full-body apparitions are extremely rare. The solidity of these images is highly variable. Some ghost hunters have seen ethereal, fully transparent forms that are barely discernible while others report ghosts who appear as solid as a living being.

WHY DO GHOSTS REMAIN IN A PARTICULAR PLACE?

Ghosts remain in a particular place because they are emotionally attached to a room, a building, activities, events, or special surroundings that profoundly affected them during their lives, or played a role in their death. A prime example is the haunted house, inhabited by the ghost of a man who hung himself in the master bedroom because his wife left him. It is widely believed that death and sudden transition from the physical world confuse a ghost. He or she remains in familiar or emotionally stabilizing surroundings to ease the strain. A place-bound ghost is most likely to occur when a violent death occurred with great emotional anguish. Ghosts may linger in a house, barn, cemetery, factory, or store waiting for a loved one or anyone familiar that might help them deal with their new level of existence. Some ghosts wander through buildings or forests, on bridges, or alongside particular sections of roads. Some await enemies seeking revenge. Others await a friend and a chance for resolution of their guilt.

UNDER WHAT CONDITIONS IS A SIGHTING MOST LIKELY?

Although ghosts may appear at any time, a sighting may occur on holidays (July 4), anniversaries, birthdays, or during historic periods (December 7, September 11), or calendar periods pertaining to the personal history of the ghost. Halloween is reputed to be a favorite night for many apparitions, while others seem to prefer their own special day, or night, on a weekly or monthly cycle.

Night is a traditional time for ghost activity, yet experienced ghost hunters know that sightings may occur at any time. There seems to be no consistent affinity of ghosts for darkness, but they seldom appear when artificial light is bright. Perhaps this is why ghosts shy away from camera crews and their array of lights. Ghosts seem to prefer peace and quiet, although some of them have been reported to make incessant, loud sounds. Even a small group of ghost hunters may make too much noise to facilitate a sighting. For this reason, it is recommended that you limit your group to four people and keep oral communication to a minimum.

IS GHOST HUNTING DANGEROUS?

Ghost hunting is not dangerous. Motion pictures and children's ghost stories have created a widespread notion that ghosts may inflict harm or even cause the death of people they dislike. There are a few reports of ghosts attacking people but these are highly suspect. People who claim to have been injured by a ghost have, in most cases, precipitated the injury themselves through their own ignorance or fear. The ghost of the Abbot of Trondheim was reputed to have attacked some people decades ago, but circumstances and precipitating events are unclear. Authorities believe that rare attacks by ghosts are a matter of mistaken identity—the ghost misidentified a living person as a figure known to the ghost during his life.

It is possible that attacks may be nothing more than clumsy efforts by a ghost to achieve recognition. Witnesses of ghost appearances have found themselves in the middle of gunfights, major military battles, and other violent events yet sustained not the slightest injury. If the ghost hunter keeps a wary eye and a calm attitude and sets aside tendencies to fear the ghost or the circumstances of its appearance, he will be safe.

Most authorities agree that ghosts do not travel. Ghosts will not follow you home, take up residence in your car, or attempt to occupy your body. They are held in time and space by deep emotional ties to an event or place. Ghosts have been observed on airplanes, trains, buses, and ships. However, it is unlikely that the destination interests them. Something about the journey—some event such as a plane crash or train wreck—accounts for their appearance as travelers.

HOT SPOTS FOR GHOSTLY ACTIVITY

Numerous sites of disasters, criminal activity, suicides, huge fires, and other tragic events abound in New Orleans and south Louisiana, providing hundreds of opportunities for ghost hunting. You may visit the locations described in chapters 2 through 5 to experience ghostly activity discovered by others or discover a hot spot to research and initiate your own ghost hunt.

Astute ghost hunters often search historical maps, drawings, and other documents to find the sites of military conflicts, buildings that no longer exist, or tragic events now occupied by modern structures. For example, maps and drawings on display in museums, plantation mansions, and other historic locations may point to the former location of houses, churches, schools, or graves that may be under parking lots, streets, or other structures. At historic places such as the

Louisiana State Museum in the Old U.S. Mint, the Cabildo at Jackson Square, and Jackson Barracks near Chalmette, old photographs can help you locate the former sites of canals, slave quarters, barns, barracks for soldiers, and other places to stage a ghost hunt.

Fires and hurricanes have resulted in a large number of sudden and tragic deaths in New Orleans. In 1788, a huge fire swept through New Orleans, destroying hundreds of homes and killing many unfortunate souls who could not outrace the flames and smoke. Another major fire occurred in 1794 killing more than a hundred people and destroying buildings that had been constructed with blood, sweat, and tears, mostly by local slaves. In 1794 three hurricanes struck the city, displacing thousands and killing hundreds of people. Those who died in these disasters, or their aftermath, may haunt the site of their cherished homes, favorite bars or restaurants, or workplaces.

Many churches exist throughout New Orleans and south Louisiana, with structures dating from the mid-1700s. Most of them, such as St. Louis Cathedral on Jackson Square and St. Mary's Church at the Ursuline Convent, are beautifully restored and open to the public. The sanctuaries and grounds of these magnificent places of worship contain graves of well-known Catholic priests, in addition to mass graves of those who died in the epidemics of the 19th century.

In the French Quarter, the homes of many well-known residents, such as Mayor Nicholas Girod's Napoleon House on Chartres Street, the Beauregard-Keyes House also on Chartres Street, and the Louis and Delphine Lalaurie mansion on Royal Street, are reputed to harbor ghosts. Outside the French Quarter, historic homes such as the Pitot House on Moss Street and Magnolia Mansion in the Garden District have curious histories and ghostly atmospheres. Up the Mississippi River, popular destinations for ghost hunters include plantations such as Nottoway in White Castle, Loyd Hall in Opelousas, and Houmas House near Burnside on the famous River Road. Downriver from New Orleans, the Woodland Plantation house, at West Point a la Heche, has a ghostly history. Of course, St. Francisville's world-famous Myrtles Plantation is well known for ghostly activity. Some of these charming old homes have become bed-and-breakfast inns, museums, or restaurants, making them exciting weekend destinations for ghost hunters.

Several historic military sites in south Louisiana are believed to harbor ghosts. These include Chalmette Battlefield and National Cemetery, site of the historic Battle of New Orleans in 1815, Fort Pike on the shores of Lake Pontchartrain, and the Armory at Jackson Barracks.

Many cemeteries dating from the 18th century are scattered about New Orleans, many of them with fascinating lists of occupants, epitaphs, and architecture. These cities of the dead are composed mostly of above-ground tombs and crypts because much of New Orleans is below sea level.

St. Louis Cemetery Number 1 contains tombs of several fascinating people, among them voodoo priestess Marie Laveau. Her grave is decorated with offerings—bottles of rum, beads, flowers, bones, bags of powdered substances, crosses, and coins—left by voodoo followers and others fascinated with her history and mystical religion. Marie's tomb is decorated by hundreds of *X*s scratched with brick shards as a prelude to making a wish of the long-deceased voodoo priestess.

At Metairie Cemetery, the templelike tomb of New Orleans' most famous madam, Josie Arlington, can be found. The architecture of this grand structure includes carved granite flames. Soon after Arlington's burial, local residents were horrified to see them burning brightly through the night. Also, the life-size bronze statue of a young woman—one of Josie's girls—reaching for the door handle created several local legends and ghost stories.

The best way to see New Orleans' famed cemeteries and learn fascinating histories of those entombed is to tour them with a knowledgeable guide. (See Appendix F: Special Tours and Events.) These places are too spooky and unsafe after dark unless you are with people who can insure a pleasant visit.

TWO SIMPLE RULES

Two simple rules apply for successful ghost hunting. The first is to be patient. Ghosts are everywhere, but contact may require a considerable investment of time. The second rule is to have fun.

You may report your ghost-hunting experiences or suggest hot spots for ghost hunting to the author via e-mail at Ghosthunter@JeffDwyer.com. Visit the Author's Web site at www.jeffdwyer.com.

Ghost Hunter's Guide
to
New Orleans

CHAPTER 1

How to Hunt for Ghosts

You may want to visit recognized haunted sites, listed in chapters 2 through 5, using some of the ghost-hunting techniques described later in this chapter. Or you may want to conduct your own spirit investigation. If that is the case, choose a place you think might be haunted, like an old house in your neighborhood or a favorite bed-and-breakfast inn. You may get a lead from fascinating stories about ancestors that have been passed down through your family.

Your search for a ghost, or exploration of a haunted place, starts with research. Summaries of obscure and esoteric material about possible haunted sites are available from museums, local historical societies, and bookstores. Brochures and booklets, sold at historical sites under the Louisiana State Park system, can be good resources, too.

Guided tours of historical sites, such as the Garden District, Jackson Square, old churches, or New Orleans' famous cemeteries, are good places to begin your research. Tours can help you develop a feel for places within a building where ghosts might be or an appreciation of relevant history. New Orleans ghost, cemetery, and vampire tours are very popular and offer a good way to learn a lot about local paranormal activity in a short time.

In addition, touring haunted buildings offers you an opportunity to speak with guides and docents who may be able to provide you with clues about the dearly departed or tell you ghost stories you can't find in published material. Docents may know people—old-timers in the area or amateur historians—who can give you additional information about a site, its former owners or residents, and its potential for ghostly activity.

Almost every city has a local historical society. (See Appendix G.) These are good places to find information that may not be published anywhere else, including histories of local families and buildings, information about tragedies, disasters, criminal activity, or legends and myths about places that may be haunted. Take notes about secret scandals or other ghost-producing happenings that occurred at locations now occupied by modern buildings, roads, or parks. In these cases, someone occupying a new house or other structure may be hearing strange sounds, feeling cold spots, or seeing ghosts or spirit remnants.

Newspapers are an excellent source of historical information as well. You can search for articles about ghosts, haunted places, or paranormal activity by accessing the newspaper's archives via the Internet and entering key words, dates, or names. Newspaper articles about suicides, murders, train wrecks, plane crashes, and paranormal phenomena can often provide essential information for your ghost hunt. Stories about authentic haunted sites are common around Halloween. Bookstores and libraries usually have special-interest sections with books on local history by local writers. A few inquiries may connect you with these local writers who may be able to help you focus your research.

If these living souls cannot help, try the dead. A visit to a local graveyard is always fruitful in identifying possible ghosts. Often you can find headstones that indicate the person entombed died of suicide, criminal activity, local disaster, or such. Some epitaphs may indicate if the deceased was survived by a spouse and children or died far from home.

Perhaps the best place to start a search for a ghost is within your own family. Oral histories can spark your interest in a particular ancestor, scandal, building, or site relevant to your family. Old photographs, death certificates, letters, wills, anniversary lists in family Bibles, and keepsakes can be great clues. Then you can visit gravesites and/or homes of your ancestors to check out the vibes as you mentally and emotionally empathize with specific aspects of your family's history.

Almost every family has a departed member who died at an early age, suffered hardships and emotional anguish, passed away suddenly due to an accident or natural disaster, or was labeled a skeleton in the family's closet. Once you have focused your research on a deceased person, you need to determine if that person remains on this earthly plane as a ghost. Evaluate the individual's personal history to see if he had a reason to remain attached to a specific place.

Was his death violent or under tragic circumstances?
Did he die at a young age with unfinished business?
Did the deceased leave behind loved ones who needed his support and protection?
Was this person attached to a specific site or building?
Would the individual be inclined to seek revenge against those responsible for his death?
Would his devotion and sense of loyalty lead him to offer eternal companionship to loved ones?

Revenge, anger, refusal to recognize the reality of transformation by death, and other negative factors prompt many spirits to haunt places and people. However, most ghosts are motivated by positive factors. Spirits may remain at a site to offer protection to a loved one or a particular place.

Also, remember that ghosts can appear as animals or objects. Apparitions of ships, buildings, covered wagons, bridges, and roads by the strictest definitions, are phantoms. A phantom is the essence of a structure that no longer exists on the physical plane. Many people have seen houses, cottages, castles, villages, and large ships that were destroyed or sunk years before.

BASIC PREPARATION FOR GHOST HUNTING

If you decide to ghost hunt at night, or on a special anniversary, make a trip to the site a few days ahead of time. During daylight hours, familiarize yourself with the place and its surroundings. Many historical sites are closed after sunset or crowded at certain times by organized tours.

TWO BASIC METHODS FOR FINDING GHOSTS

Based partly on the kind of paranormal activity reported at a site, the ghost hunter must decide which method or approach will be used.

Some people feel competent with a collection of cameras, electromagnetic field detectors, digital thermometers, computers, data recorders, and other high-tech gadgets. These ghost hunters prefer to use the Technical Approach. Others may discover they have an emotional affinity for a particular historic location, experience a surprising fascination with an event associated with a haunting, or feel empathy for a deceased person. These ghost hunters may have success with the Psychic Approach. Another consideration is the ghost hunter's goal. Some desire scientific evidence of a ghost while others simply want to experience paranormal activity.

THE TECHNICAL APPROACH

Professional ghost hunters often use an array of detection and recording devices that cover a wide range of the electromagnetic spectrum. This approach is complicated, expensive, and requires technically skilled people to operate the devices. Amateur ghost hunters can get satisfying results with simple audio and video recording devices.

Equipment Preparation

A few days before your ghost hunt, purchase fresh film for your camera and tape for audio recording devices. Test your batteries and bring back-up batteries and power packs with you. You should have two types of flashlights: a broad-beam light for moving around a site and a penlight-type flashlight for narrow-field illumination while you make notes or adjust equipment. A candle is a good way to light the site that is least offensive to your ghost.

Still-Photography Techniques

Many photographic techniques that work well under normal conditions are inadequate for ghost hunts because they are usually conducted under conditions of low ambient light requiring long exposures. Some investigators use a strobe or flash device, but they can make the photos look unauthentic.

Practice taking photographs with films of various light sensitivities before you go on your ghost hunt. Standard photographic films of high light sensitivity should be used—ASA of 800 or higher is recommended. At a dark or nearly dark location, mount the camera on a tripod. Try several exposure settings from one to 30 seconds and aperture settings under various low-light conditions.

Make notes about the camera settings that work best under various light conditions. Avoid aiming the camera at a scene where there is a bright light, such as a street lamp or exit sign over a doorway. These light sources may "overflow" throughout your photograph.

Some professional ghost hunters use infrared film. You should consult a professional photo lab technician about this type of film and its associated photographic techniques. Several amateur ghost hunters use Polaroid-type cameras with interesting results. The rapid film developing system used by these cameras gives almost instant feedback about your technique and/or success in documenting ghost activities. Ghosts have reportedly written messages on Polaroid film.

Many digital cameras have features that enable automatic exposures at specific intervals, such as once every minute. This allows a hands-off remote photograph to be made. Repetitive automatic exposures also allow a site to be investigated without the presence of the investigator.

Your equipment should include a stable, light-weight tripod. Hand-held cameras may produce poorly focused photographs when the exposure duration is greater that $\frac{1}{60}$ second.

Audio Recording Techniques

Tape recorders provide an inexpensive way to obtain evidence of ghostly activity, particularly electronic voice phenomenon or EVP. Always test your recorder under conditions you expect to find at the investigation site to reduce audio artifact and insure optimal performance of the device. If your recorder picks up excessive background noise, this may obscure ghostly sounds. Consider upgrading the tape quality and use a microphone equipped with a wind guard. Use two or more recorders at different locations within the site. This allows you to verify sounds such as wind against a window and reduce the possibility of ambiguous recordings.

You can use sound-activated recorders at a site over night. They automatically switch on whenever a sound occurs above a minimum threshold. Be aware that each sound on the tape will start with an annoying artifact, the result of a slow tape speed at the beginning of each recorded segment. The slow tape speed could obscure the sounds made by a ghost.

Remote microphones and monitor earphones allow you to remain some distance from the site and activate the recorder when ghostly sounds are heard. If this equipment is not available, use long-play tape (60-90 minutes), turn the recorder on, and let it run throughout your hunt, whether you remain stationary or walk about the site. This allows you to make audio notes rather than written notes. A headset with a microphone is especially useful with this technique.

Video Recording

Video recorders offer a wide variety of recording features from time lapse to auto start/stop, and auto focus. These features enable you to make surveillance-type recordings over many hours while you are off site. Consult your user's manual for low-light recording guidelines and always use a tripod and long-duration battery packs.

If you plan to attempt video recording, consider using two recorders, at equal distances from a specific object such as a chair. Arrange the recorders at different angles, preferably 90 degrees from each other.

Another approach you might try is to use a wide-angle setting on the first camera to get a broad view of a room, porch, or courtyard, and on the second camera, use a close-up setting to capture ghostly apparitions at a door, chair, or window.

You may have more success with sequential, manual, or timer-actuated tape runs than a continuous-record technique. If you try this technique, use tape runs of one to five minutes. Practice with the method that interrupts the automatic setting should you need to manually control the recording process. Always use a tripod that can be moved to a new location in a hurry.

High-Tech Equipment

Night-vision goggles can be useful in low-light situations. You can see doors and other objects move that you might not otherwise see. These goggles are quite expensive, however. You can also buy devices such as electromagnetic field detectors, infrared thermometers, barometers, and motion detectors at your local electronics store or over the Internet. A good source for high-tech ghost-hunting equipment is www.technica.com. Electronic gadgets can be useful and fun, but unless you have a means of recording the output, your reports of anomalies, movement, and apparitions will not be the kind of hard evidence you need to satisfy skeptics.

Other Equipment

Various authorities in the field of ghost hunting suggest the following items to help you mark sites, detect paranormal phenomena, and collect evidence of ghostly activity:

White or colored chalk
Compass
Stopwatch
Steel tape measure
Magnifying glass
First-aid kit
Thermometer
Metal detector
Graph paper for diagrams
Small mirror
Small bell
Plastic bags for collecting evidence
Matches
Tape for sealing doors
String
A cross
A Bible
Mobile phone

THE PSYCHIC APPROACH

The Psychic Approach relies upon your intuition, inner vision, or emotional connection with a deceased person, an object, a place, or a point of time in history. You don't have to be a trained psychic to use this approach. All of us have some capacity to tap into unseen dimensions.

People who feel the peculiar atmosphere of a distant time or believe they can perceive a voice, sound, image, touch, or texture of another dimension may have psychic abilities that will pay off in a ghost hunt. The Psychic Approach does require an ability to eliminate external and internal distractions and focus your perceptions. If you use this approach, three factors may increase your chances of experiencing ghostly activity.

The first factor is the strength of the emotional imprint or attachment the deceased has for a particular place. The frequency, duration, and consistency of the paranormal phenomena may indicate this. The strongest imprints are created by intense emotions such as fear, rage, jealously, revenge, or loss, especially if they were repetitive over long periods of time prior to death. Other emotions such as love for a person, a place, or an object may also create a strong imprint. Biographical research may reveal this kind of information, particularly if personal letters or diaries are examined. Old newspaper articles and photographs are useful, too.

The second factor is the degree of sensitivity the investigator has for environmental imprints. Knowledge of the key elements and historical context of the entity's death can increase your sensitivity. This includes architectural elements of a home, a theater, an airplane, a ship, furniture, clothing, weapons, or any implement or artifact of the specific time period. Touching or handling these artifacts, or standing within the historic site, enables ghost hunters to get in touch with the historical moment of the ghost's imprint. A high degree of sensitivity for a past era often generates an odd feeling of being transported through time.

The third factor is sensitivity to or empathy for the ghost's lingering presence at a haunted site. A ghost may be trapped, confused, or choose to remain at a site to protect someone or guard something precious. Sensitivity for the ghost's predicament can be increased through knowledge of the entity's personal history such as emotions, motivations, problems, or unfinished business at the time of death. Research of historical sources like newspapers, old photographs, or books can provide this kind of information. Useful, intimate details might be found in letters, suicide notes, diaries, and wills.

Your sensitivity to ghostly environmental imprints and spirit manifestations may be increased by meditation. This is a simple process of relaxing your physical body to eliminate distracting thoughts and tensions and achieve emotional focus. Meditation allows you to focus your spiritual awareness on a single subject: a place, an entity, or a historic moment in time. As the subject comes into focus, you can add information obtained from your research. Markers of time or seasons, artifacts or implements, furniture, and doorways are a few suggestions. By doing this, you become aware of unseen dimensions of the world around you that create a feeling that you have moved through time to a distant era. This process gets you in touch with the place, date, and time pertinent to a ghost's imprint or death. It also enables you to disregard personal concerns and distracting thoughts that may interfere with your concentration on the ghost you seek.

Keep in mind that it is possible to be in a meditative state while appearing quite normal. The process is simple and easy to learn. When you arrive at the site of your ghost hunt, find a place a short distance away to meditate. Three essentials for any effective meditation are comfort, quiet, and concentration.

Comfort: Sit or stand in a relaxed position. Take free and even breaths at a slow rate. Do not alter your breathing pattern so much that you feel short of breath, winded, or lightheaded. Close your eyes, if that enhances your comfort, or focus on a candle, tree, or flower. Do not fall asleep. Proper meditation creates relaxation without decreasing alertness.

Quiet: Meditate in a place away from noises generated by traffic, passersby, radios, slammed doors, and the like. If you are with a group, give each other sufficient personal space. Some people use mantras, repetitive words or phrases, or speak only in their mind in order to facilitate inner calmness. Mantras are useful to induce a focused state of relaxation, but they may disrupt the meditation of a companion if spoken aloud. A majority of ghost hunters do not believe that mantras are necessary in this instance. They point out that ghost hunting is not like a séance as depicted in old movies. It is not necessary to chant special words, call out to the dead, or invite an appearance "from beyond the grave."

Concentration: First, clear your mind of everyday thoughts, worries, and concerns. This is the most difficult part of the process. Many people don't want to let go of their stressful thoughts. To help you let go of those thoughts, let the thought turn off its light and fade into darkness. After you clear your mind, some thoughts may reappear. Repeat the process. Slowly turn off the light of each thought until you can rest with a completely cleared mind. This might take some practice. Don't wait until you are on the scene of a ghost hunt before you practice this exercise.

Once your mind is clear, focus on your breathing and imagine your entire being as a single point of energy driving the breathing process. Then, open yourself, thinking only of the entity you seek. Starting with the ghost's identity (if known), slowly expand your focus to include its personal history, the historical era of the ghost's death or creation of the emotional imprint, the reported nature and appearance of the haunting, and any specific ghostly activity.

Acknowledge each thought as you continue relaxed breathing. Find a thought that is most attractive to you, and then expand your mind to include your present surroundings. Return slowly to your current place and time. Remain quiet for a minute or two before you resume communication with your companions, then move ahead with the ghost hunt.

GROUP ORGANIZATION AND PREPARATION

It is not necessary to be a believer in spirits or paranormal phenomena in order to see a ghost or experience haunting activities. Indeed, most reports of ghost activities are made by unsuspecting people who never gave the matter much thought. But you should not include people in your group with openly negative attitudes about these things. If you include skeptics, be sure they maintain an open mind and are willing to participate in a positive group attitude.

Keep your group small, limited to four members if possible. Ghosts have been seen by large groups of people but small groups are more easily managed and likely to be of one mind in terms of objectives and methods.

Meet an hour or more prior to starting the ghost hunt at a location away from the site. Review the history of the ghost you seek and the previous reports of ghost activity at the site. Discuss the group's expectations based on known or suspected ghostly activity or specific research goals. Review possible audio and visual apparitions based on the history of paranormal activity at the site, telekinesis, local temperature changes, and intended methods of identifying or recording these phenomena. Most important, agree to a plan of action if a sighting is made by any member of the group.

The first priority for a ghost hunter is to maintain visual or auditory contact without a lot of activity such as making notes. Without breaking contact, do the following:

- activate recording devices
- redirect audio, video, or photographic equipment to focus on the ghost
- move yourself to the most advantageous position for listening or viewing the ghostly activity
- attract the attention of group members with a code word, hand signal (touch the top of your head), or any action that signals other hunters so they can pick up your focus of attention

Only attempt to interact with a ghost if it invites you to speak or move. Often, ghost hunters' movement or noise frightens a ghost or interferes with the perception of the apparition.

SEARCHING FOR GHOSTS

There are no strict rules or guidelines for successful ghost hunting except to be patient. Professional ghost hunters sometimes wait several days, weeks, or even months before achieving contact with a ghost. Others have observed full-body apparitions when they least expected them, while concentrating fully on some other activity. Regardless of the depth of your research or preparation, you need to be patient. A serious ghost hunter should anticipate that several trips to a haunted site may be required before some sign of ghostly activity is observed.

If you hunt with a group, you need to establish a communications system in the event that even one member might sight a ghost or experiences some evidence of ghostly activity. Of course, confirmation by a second person is important in establishing validity and credibility. In the previous section, a hand signal (hand to the top of the head) was recommended as a means of informing others that they should direct their eyes and ears to a site indicated by the person in contact with a ghost. Because of this, all ghost hunters need to keep their companions in sight at all times and be aware of hand signals.

An audio signal can often reduce the need for monitoring other ghost hunters for hand signals. Equally important for a group is to establish a method for calling other hunters who may be some distance away. Tugging on a length of string can be an effective signal, as can beeping devices, mechanical "crickets," and flashing penlight signals, such as one flash for a cold spot and two flashes for an apparition. Hand-held radios, or walkie-talkies, can also be effective. Some models can send an audio signal or activate flashing lights. Cell phones can be used but the electromagnetic activity may be uninviting to your ghost.

Remaining stationary within a room, gravesite, courtyard, or other confirmed location is often most productive. If a ghost is known to have a favorite chair, bed, or other place within a room, it will appear. Under these conditions, the patient ghost hunter may have a successful hunt.

If your ghost is not known to appear at a specific place within a room or an outdoor area, position yourself to gain the broadest view of the site. A corner of a room is optimal because it allows the ghost unobstructed motion about the place while avoiding the impression of a trap set by uninvited people who occupy its favorite space. If you are outdoors at a gravesite, for instance, position yourself at the base of a tree or in the shadows of a monument to conceal your presence while affording a view of your ghost's grave.

If your ghost is a mobile spirit, moving throughout a house, over a bridge, or about a courtyard or graveyard, you may have no choice but to move around the area. Search for a place where you sense a change in the thickness of the air, feel a cold spot, or detect a peculiar odor. If you are ghost hunting with others, it may be advantageous to station members of your group at various places in the ghost's haunting grounds and use a reliable system to alert others to spirit activity. Each member could then patrol a portion of the site. Radio or mobile-phone communications may be essential for this type of ghost hunt.

Once you are on site, the above-described meditation may help you focus and maintain empathy for your ghost. Investigate sounds, even common sounds, as the ghost attempts to communicate with you. Make mental notes of the room temperature, air movement, and the sensations of abrupt change in atmosphere as you move about the site. Changes in these factors may indicate the presence of a ghost. Pay attention to your own sensations or perceptions, such as the odd feeling that someone is watching you, standing close by, or touching you. Your ghost may be hunting you!

WHAT TO DO WITH A GHOST

On occasion, professional ghost hunters make contact with ghosts by entering a trance and establishing two-way communications. The ghost hunter's companions hear him or her speak, but the ghost's voice can only be heard by the trance communicator. Sylvia Browne's book *Adventures of a Psychic* describes several of these trance communication sessions. However, most ghost encounters are brief with little opportunity to engage the entity in conversation. A ghost may make gestures or acknowledge your presence through eye contact, a touch on the shoulder, sound, or a movement of an object. The ghost hunter must decide to follow the gestures or direction of a ghost or not.

Visitors to south Louisiana plantations and historic French Quarter buildings often feel the touch or tug of ghosts on their arms or shoulders. These ghosts may be trying to get living souls to notice them, move out of their way, or follow them to some important destination. A ghost at Destrehan Plantation, believed to be the pirate Jean Lafitte, points to locations in the kitchen where treasure may be hidden. Ghosts who wander the levees along the Mississippi sometimes wave to people driving the River Road, beckoning them to follow. People who are brave enough to stick their hands through the tiny, barred windows of the slave quarters behind Keuffers building on Chartres Street in the French Quarter may feel the hands of slave children who died 150 years ago during an epidemic. These poor souls may want you to pull them out or enter the dark rooms and rescue them.

At the former O'Flaherty's Irish Channel Pub on Toulouse Street, the ghost of murderer Joseph Baptandiere has grabbed the forearms of ghost hunters, creating visible impressions. One visitor felt an invisible rope tighten around her neck that left red marks. In 1810, Baptandiere killed himself by tying a rope around his neck and dropping out of a third floor window above O'Flaherty's pub.

To date, there are no reports of lasting ill effects by those who have been brave enough to follow these spirits or experienced contact with them. Residents of haunted houses and employees of haunted business establishments often accept ghosts' telekinetic or audio activities without concern. It is part of the charm of a place and may add some fun to working in a spooky building.

Experiences such as these are frightening to most of us. More often, the ghost's activities are directed at getting the intruder to leave a room, house, or gravesite. If you sense your ghost wants you to leave, most hunters believe it is best not to push your luck. When you have established the nature of the ghost activity, ascertained that your companions have experienced the activity, made a few photographs and run a few minutes of audio tape, it may be time to leave. An experience with an unfriendly ghost can be disturbing.

AFTER THE GHOST HUNT

Turn off all recorders and remove them to a safe place. Some ghost hunters suspect that ghosts can erase tapes. Label your tapes with the date, time, and location. Use a code number for each tape. Keep a separate record of where the tape was made, as well as the date, time, and contents. Place tapes in a waterproof bag with your name, address, telephone number, and a note that guarantees postage in case it is misplaced. Have photographic film developed at a professional color laboratory. Pros at the lab may help you with cropping and image enhancement. Have copies made of any negatives that contain ghostly images.

All members of the group should meet right after the hunt away from the site. Each hunter who witnessed ghostly activity or an apparition should make a written or audio statement describing the experience. The form, presented in Appendix A, is for the group leader to complete. Video and audio recordings made at the site should be reviewed and reconciled with witness statements. Plans should be made for a follow-up visit in the near future to the site to confirm the apparition, its nature and form, and the impressions of the initial ghost hunt.

Data about the ghost's location within a site may indicate the optimal conditions for future contact. Things to be aware of include the time of day or night, phase of the moon, season, degree and size of cold spots, as well as form and density of the apparition. Patience and detailed records can help you to achieve the greatest reward for a ghost hunter—unmistakable proof of ghostly activity.

CHAPTER 2

The Garden District and Uptown

Soon after the Louisiana Purchase of 1803, Americans began a steady migration from northern states to the low country to take advantage of the booming commerce along the Mississippi River. Upon entering the old French Quarter, however, they were viewed by the Creoles and Spanish as interlopers who lacked social graces and had no appreciation for the New Orleans way of doing business. Friction was so great that many newcomers moved out of the Quarter and established a new American neighborhood that would be known as the Garden District.

The former Livaudais Plantation, upriver from New Orleans, was subdivided and incorporated as the city of Lafayette. Opulent mansions and ornate gardens were built on wide streets to arouse the envy of the crowded residents of the Vieux Carré and show off the new wealth of the Americans. By 1850, frictions had dissipated, and Lafayette was absorbed into New Orleans.

MAGNOLIA MANSION

2127 Prytania Street
New Orleans 70130
504-412-9500
www.magnoliamansion.com

This beautiful antebellum mansion is haunted. Ask anyone in the neighborhood or go to the Web site and read statements by guests who experienced the ghostly activity that has made this place famous.

The hauntings may be linked to a strange coincidence. Funerals for two owners were staged in the mansion after each lived there about ten years. Both were married to domineering women named Lizzie. Another ghost is believed to be the spirit of a teenage girl who lived across the street.

The Magnolia Mansion was constructed in 1858 as a wedding gift from Alexander Harris to his teenage bride, Lizzie. Harris made his fortune in the cotton brokerage business. He died on July 19, 1869, probably of yellow fever. It is strange that his death occurred about 24 hours after the death of his brother and business partner, Aaron. Within months, Alexander's widow, Lizzie, gained control of his fortune and filed a lawsuit against Aaron's widow, which resulted in the eviction of her sister-in-law and her five children. Less than two years later, she married Carneal Burke. Added to that, Lizzie did not make a will or deed the mansion to her children, but sold it, making the proceeds part of the Burke estate. Viewing all of this from the other side must have disturbed Alexander. As a result, his ghost has latched onto his beloved mansion. He watches over the guests and staff, perhaps seeking revenge if Lizzie returns.

In 1879, John Henry MacGinnis purchased the house from Lizzie Harris Burke and moved in with his wife, Lizzie, and their three children. But ten years later, MacGinnis was struck by lightning and died. His funeral was staged in the same room used for Alexander Harris's funeral. Strong of will, smart, and capable, Lizzie MacGinnis kept the family together, did not remarry, and willed her estate to her daughter, Josephine. Unlike Lizzie Harris, Lizzie MacGinnis passed the property to her daughter who retained it until 1939. The ghosts of John and Lizzie MacGinnis may roam the hallways and parlor of their mansion.

The third ghost that haunts Magnolia Mansion is that of a teenage girl named Musey. Musey lived across the street and was known in the neighborhood as a troubled teen. Musey killed herself by lying in the path of the St. Charles streetcar. It is said that the wheels of the streetcar ran over her head. Musey's ghost returned home, but when the building was demolished, she moved across the street to the more appealing Magnolia Mansion. Being a troubled personality, Musey created all kinds of disturbances when the mansion underwent major renovation. Workers reported electrical problems, doors slamming, cold gusts of air, and a strange oily substance dripping from the walls. At one point, things got so bad that workmen refused to enter the house.

Guests of this famous inn have posted several reports of ghostly activity on the Web site. Photographs and digital images have captured orbs and clouds of white light both inside and outside the mansion. Guest reports describe disembodied footsteps, sensations of a hand gripping their wrists, a cheek brushed by a cold hand, soft notes from a music box, the apparition of a little girl watching over a couple in bed, movement of objects such as glasses and keys, and disembodied hands tucking the blankets for a warm night's sleep. One guest added, "The ghosts were very polite and friendly."

BUCKNER MANSION

Mr. Charles Zambito, owner
Jackson Avenue at Coliseum
New Orleans 70130
504-524-6954

In 1853, Henry Sullivan Buckner commissioned architect Lewis E. Reynolds to build the largest house in the district. The result was a home of more than 20,000 square feet with 16-foot ceilings, 48 magnificent columns, and double galleries that wrap around three sides of the structure. Behind the house, a large slave quarters housed the staff required to maintain such a huge estate.

Miss Josephine ran the house. A free woman of color, Miss Josephine was in charge of all the house slaves, livery boys, gardeners, and kitchen slaves. She was a demanding mistress, making sure every job was done right, without delay or mishap, and all the slaves were properly dressed. Miss Josephine even served as midwife, birthing many babies in the slave quarters behind the great house. When the delivery went badly, she nursed the mother back to health and buried the newborn. Miss Josephine was so capable and trusted that she also acted as governess for the Buckners' children. The lady was so devoted to the house and the Buckner family that she stayed on after the

Civil War when all the freed slaves left town. When Josephine died, her body was buried in Lafayette Cemetery Number 1, but her ghost returned to work, managing the Buckner estate on beautiful Jackson Avenue.

The sound of Miss Josephine's broom is still heard in several rooms. This sound appears to be a remnant of the housekeeper's habit of going from room to room, whisking the floors and carpets to add a final, personal touch before the Buckner family entertained guests. Miss Josephine also effuses her favorite lemon scent as she passes through the rooms of the mansion. Several witnesses have seen the counterweights on chandeliers swing for more than an hour, lights flash on and off, and doors swing open.

Miss Josephine has also been seen from Coliseum Street by ghost hunters and passersby. This side street offers a view of both the mansion's rear galleries and the galleries of the three-story slave quarters.

The ghost of house mistress Miss Josephine has been seen on the rear galleries of the Buckner Mansion.

Her partial apparition has been spotted walking the galleries and climbing the stairs. Several people have seen her gazing out the windows at the street. Psychic investigators who have entered Josephine's room report the sounds of women praying and an atmosphere of profound sadness. One psychic burst into tears as she became aware that many young lives had ended in the room. This may be the environmental imprint left by the several slave women who died in childbirth.

Today, the Buckner Mansion can be rented for parties, weddings, or as long-term accommodations for large groups, such as movie crews or corporate groups on retreat. The spacious rooms are furnished in antebellum elegance. Every room looks as though the staff continues to meet Miss Josephine's high standards.

HOUSE OF THE VOODOO RITUAL

1331 First Street
New Orleans 70130

The iron balustrades and mauve paint job make this house look solid, calm, and almost sedate among the other Victorian mansions that line First Street. Built in 1868 by a successful merchant, its large rooms and galleries no doubt housed several families over the past 135 years. Looking at the conservative architecture, it is easy to assume its occupants were proper, conservative Yankees enjoying asylum from the flamboyant residents of the neighboring French Quarter. But a discovery was made here a few years ago that casts a new light on this mansion.

During extensive renovations, a small room was discovered. Fancy woodwork, including chair rails, heavy moldings, and door frames conspired with the angles of the walls to conceal the space. When workmen removed plaster, the secret space was exposed, revealing dust, paint colors, and other clues indicating the space had not been opened for decades, perhaps a century. This fascinating discovery took a strange twist when the floorboards were pulled up. In a space measuring three feet square, workmen discovered a human skull and two femurs, or thigh bones. The femurs were crossed under the skull creating the Jolly Roger symbol usually seen on pirate flags in movies. Old New Orleans was often visited by pirates, but it is believed that the bones arranged in this design were used in a voodoo ritual.

The skull was examined by experts and found to be from an adolescent, possibly deformed. Only one of the femurs came from this individual. The other is of similar size and is believed to have come from a person of similar size, age, and sex. It is not known what kind of voodoo ritual would have used human bones such as these, placed in this particular pattern. It has been suggested that these bones may be the remnants of a vampire ritual instead. There is little historical information to go on, but real bones placed to resemble the traditional pirate's symbol may have been used to frighten away vampires. Garlic, crosses, and sunlight also keep them at bay.

Ghost hunters who visit this house at night have captured orbs on film and digital media. Orbs tend to accumulate near the ground, in large numbers, as if guarding the foundation and underground approaches to the house. Streaks of pale light have also shown up in photographs.

If you look at the ceiling over the porch, you'll see that it is painted sky blue. Many houses in the Garden District have this same feature, created to protect against evil or frighten unwanted spirits. It was once believed that if these spirits, roaming the neighborhood at night, walked or floated onto the porch and looked upward, they would see what looked like a pale blue sky typical of a Louisiana afternoon in springtime. Since no self-respecting ghosts would haunt the living in daytime, the spirits would slip away, leaving the family undisturbed within the house.

JEFFERSON DAVIS DEATH HOUSE

2362 Camp Street (at First Street)
New Orleans 70130

Passersby, Garden District tour groups, and residents of the neighborhood often spot a man gazing out a second-floor window of this house. He appears old and gray, with a short beard, uncombed hair, and prominent cheek bones. The man appears surprised by what he

Evidence of voodoo rituals has been uncovered at this Garden District mansion on First Street

sees in the street and pleased to see blue sky overhead. His head and shoulders are visible only for a few seconds before they vanish. When he is not at the window, this ghost walks the floors of the house asking, "Where are my boots?"

Given the history of this house, there is little doubt as to the identity of this ghost. He is the former president of the Confederate States of America, the honorable Jefferson Davis. Records show that Davis died in this house at 1:00 A.M. on December 5, 1889. Further confirmation of the ghost's identity is derived from his published statement that he did not want to die with his boots off.

Jefferson Davis's ghost has been sought in many locations. His apparition has been sighted near his grave in Richmond, Virginia; in the halls of Congress, where he served as a congressman and senator; and at the Confederate Museum in downtown New Orleans, where some of his personal belongings are on display.

After the Civil War, Davis was imprisoned in chains for two years and charged with crimes never adjudicated in a court of law despite his demands for a trial. After his release, he received an enthusiastic reception in Richmond and the Carolinas. As he continued his journey home to the Deep South, he avoided public events. By the time he established his residence on Camp Street in the Garden District, he was a recluse. It is said that in his final years, he was seldom seen outside the house, but often gazed out the windows at the busy neighborhood. His ghost seems to be at it still. If he could find his boots, he might venture outdoors to the porch.

This house is a private residence and ghost hunters should respect the privacy of its occupants. Viewing the place from the outside may be a rewarding way to hunt this ghost.

THE SUICIDE HOME OWNER

The Ann Rice House
1239 First Street
New Orleans 70115

Albert Hamilton Brevard had a taste for fine things that included wine, food, and architecture. In 1857, Brevard commissioned James

Caltow and Charles Pride to design and build the traditional house that still stands at 1239 First Street. Greek Revival and Italianate features were combined at the request of Brevard. The home included modern conveniences, such as hot and cold running water in the four bedrooms and traditional double galleries to catch cooling breezes. At its completion, the house was considered one of the finest in the Garden District.

Brevard enjoyed his wonderful home only two years before financial problems began to mount. He had paid $12,000 for construction of the house, but the local tax assessor placed a much higher value on it. Requests for reassessment were denied, and Brevard found he could not pay. In order to save his family from losing the house, he discovered a novel way of reducing its assessed value. After a relaxing walk around the galleries, Brevard positioned himself on the porch in front of the door, raised a pistol to his head, and shot himself. With this tragic act, Brevard accomplished two important things. First, he avoided spoiling the house's fine woodwork and wallpaper with his blood and brain tissue. And second, his suicide at the threshold of the home lowered the assessed value and taxes.

Brevard's daughter was able to hold onto the home until 1869, when it was sold to the Reverend Emory Clapp. This man of the cloth was able to set aside superstition and purchase the house far below its true value. He obtained the services of one of the house's original architects, Charles Pride, and expanded a first-floor room by adding hexagonal bays. After Clapp's death, his widow enclosed part of the gallery. A little more than a century later, famed writer Anne Rice purchased the property and made several modifications as well.

Brevard's tragic demise and strong attachment to his fabulous home may be why his ghost has been detected on the porch. Ghost hunters given permission to enter the property have encountered cold spots on the porch. Psychics report feelings of shame and sadness on the porch in front of the door. Ghost hunters who view the property from outside the gate find orbs in their photographs and digital images. Late on moonless nights, residents in the neighborhood sometimes see a pale mist on the porch.

Ghost hunters should note that the house is a private residence and entrance to the property is by permission only. Anne Rice and

Albert Hamilton Brevard committed suicide on the porch of this mansion, which was later occupied by novelist Anne Rice.

her family lived there from 1989 to 2004. Working in Clapp's former study, Rice wrote several books including the Mayfair Witches series. Many important details that appear in Rice's books were inspired by the house's features, including the swimming pool and the two-story side porch with its iron balconies.

THE IRISH DIGGERS

Second Street and Camp Street
New Orleans 70130

By the late 1840s, New Orleans was a true melting pot with large numbers of residents who had immigrated from Europe, the Caribbean, South America, Canada, and Africa. The increase in the city's population, from 46,000 in 1830 to more than 100,000 in 1840, included a large number of Irish immigrants. As a result of the tragic Potato Famine of the late 1840s, the Irish population of New Orleans grew by several thousand more until 1850, when one of every five residents of the Crescent City was Irish.

Contrary to a common belief, Irish immigrants did not sequester themselves in an ethnic enclave. There was no Irish Quarter or section of the city that was exclusively Irish, including the Irish Channel, which ironically was home to many German immigrants. The Irish were scattered throughout the city, employed in commerce, the professions, and as laborers. Most of the Irish immigrants who arrived after 1845 were the poor, outcast dregs of Irish society. They somehow scraped together funds to purchase a ticket to America, leaving behind the famine that gripped Ireland. They arrived ill or weakened from the arduous Atlantic crossing and penniless, with no education or job skills. So many of them died at sea that ships carrying Irish immigrants were called coffin ships.

With empty stomachs and no skills or education that would enable them to cash in on the economic boom of the growing city, the Irish had to settle for jobs as laborers. Many of these menial jobs were physically demanding and so dangerous or unhealthy that city officials and residents did not wish to use slaves to do them, which would only result in damaged goods, meaning the slave might be permanently injured, made chronically ill, or killed. As an alternative, the Irish were employed at five cents per day—enough to buy a loaf of bread. In contrast to the management of slaves, employers did not have to house, clothe, or provide medical care for their Irish workers. A nickel a day got the job done without care.

Throughout the city, but predominantly in the Garden District, Irish were put to work digging gutters to drain the streets. This backbreaking job broke the spirit of many who came to America seeking a better life. Many died in the holes and ditches they dug. With no money for burial services, hundreds of workers were buried where they fell, becoming part of the foundation of the stone-lined gutters of New Orleans. At the corner of Second and Camp streets, you can see fine examples of the square-cut gutters with stone linings built by these unfortunate souls. Under many of these are the remains of hundreds of Irish men and boys. With such an ignominious burial, some of these fellows are understandably restless.

An unknown number of Irish workers died while digging the gutters of the Garden District.

In the late evening and early morning, residents in the area often hear the ghostly sounds of shovels cutting holes and pitching gravel and soil. Many people in the area report the sound of shovels and other digging tools being dragged across the asphalt as if a group of ghost workers are walking down the street to a job site. Others have seen a strange blue mist arise from the gutters on nights when there is no moon.

THE DRINKING GHOST

Commander's Palace
1403 Washington Avenue (at Coliseum Street)
New Orleans 70130
504-899-8221
www.commanderspalace.com

Regular customers at this upscale restaurant have learned to keep an eye on their wine and liquor glasses. If left unattended, the beverage may be mysteriously consumed by an unseen entity. These and other paranormal activities are most often attributed to the restaurant's deceased founder, Emile Commander.

Commander opened this landmark restaurant in 1880 to offer fine dining to the rich folks in the Garden District. Located across the street from Lafayette Cemetery No. 1, many of Commander's first customers were families coming from visits to the graves of their loved ones. In a short time, Commander's Palace was known as one of the finest restaurants in New Orleans. The cuisine, decidedly not French, contributed much to its popularity among the American residents of the district.

During the Roaring Twenties, most of the second-floor rooms were given over to gambling and prostitution. A few private dining rooms were maintained for wealthy gentlemen who spent long hours entertaining their mistresses. While sin and debauchery were everywhere upstairs, the main dining room on the first floor was beautifully decorated and well staffed to maintain a reputation of impeccable respectability for family dining after church or visits to the cemetery.

In the 1970s, the building was renovated by the Brennan family. When the restaurant reopened, ghostly activity increased. Dishes and silverware were mysteriously rearranged or went missing, lights flashed on and off, and disembodied footsteps were heard by patrons and restaurant staff. The ghost responsible also displayed a strong affinity for alcoholic drinks. In contrast to many staff members of French Quarter restaurants, people who work at Commander's Palace decline to comment on ghostly activity. One busboy did mention that many wait staff have heard mysterious footsteps in the area where trays are loaded and in the upstairs dining room known as the Sun Porch.

The proximity of Lafayette Cemetery No. 1 to the restaurant raises the possibility that the drinking ghost of Commander's Palace was enticed to leave his or her tomb for the gaiety and fine cuisine of the restaurant. Also, the events of the 1920s may have produced a ghost or two from the illicit and dangerous activities of gamblers, con men, and prostitutes who frequented the second floor of Emile Commander's fine establishment.

LAFAYETTE CEMETERY NO. 1

Prytania Street between Washington Avenue and Sixth Street
Lafayette Cemetery Research Project
1514 Sixth Street
New Orleans 70115
504-899-1116

If this cemetery looks familiar it's because you may have seen it in several movies including *Double Jeopardy, Interview with the Vampire,* and *Dracula 2000.* Anne Rice used this "city of the dead" as a setting in many of her books. She even staged a mock funeral there to celebrate the publication of her book *Memnoch the Devil.*

Lafayette Cemetery sits on land that was once part of the Livaudais Plantation. In 1832, Madam Livaudais sold the land to developers who subdivided it and founded the city of Lafayette. The rapid influx of immigrants hastened the absorption of this little town into the bustling metropolis of New Orleans. They also provided the earliest customers for the new cemetery. By 1852, more than 2,000 victims of yellow fever, other illnesses, and accidents were interned here. The cemetery was established on a ridge that extends upriver from the

French Quarter. This high ground allowed in-ground burials that assured rapid dissipation of human remains. The decay of bones has turned the soil here—and in other New Orleans cemeteries—a chalky white. By 1860, above-ground burials were used, similar to that in other low-lying cemeteries such as St. Louis Number 1.

The Civil War brought more customers to Lafayette Cemetery No. 1, including high-ranking Confederate officers and some Yankees. The cemetery was filled to capacity by the end of the Civil War, but new burials continued as the remains of earlier internees were brushed aside. In New Orleans it has long been common practice to open a grave one year and one day after burial to remove the remains of the occupant, place them in the grave's foundation, and install a new occupant. This accounts for the long list of names—many of them unrelated—that can be seen on some tombs, crypts, and wall vaults that seem too small to house the coffins of five people or more.

The frequent opening of vaults and tombs has led to some gruesome discoveries. Some of these may be at the root of hauntings and ghostly activity that visitors have experienced at Lafayette Cemetery. On more than a few occasions, horrified family members and cemetery officials have discovered evidence that the dearly departed had not really departed before burial. The deceased was incorrectly pronounced dead when, in fact, he was in a coma. A year and a day after the funeral, when the grave was opened, the corpse was found propped up in a corner. Fingernails worn to stubs and scratches on the interior walls indicated the occupant had tried to claw his way out.

Ghost hunters who visit this cemetery in the evening have heard the sound of metal or wood scratching stone. Tapping sounds have also been reported. Cold spots close to a grave or large variations in temperature over the surface of a stone wall may indicate a good place to listen for these remnants of horrible deaths. Some ghost hunters have used stethoscopes to increase their chances of hearing a haunting created by those unfortunate souls who were buried alive.

When visiting this cemetery and others in historic New Orleans, it is a good idea to join a tour group. Knowledgeable guides provide you with a lot of information to increase your chances of experiencing something paranormal. Also, you should respect the rights and privacy of friends and family visiting the deceased.

BUSY GHOSTS

The Castle Inn
1539 Fourth Street (at St. Charles Avenue)
New Orleans 70130
504-897-0540
e-mail: castleinn@worldnet.com
www.castleinnofneworleans.com

Standing on the curb, looking at this stately mansion, you get the impression it is haunted. The dark windows, high peaked roof, and Victorian architecture bring to mind places seen in scary movies. As you climb the concrete steps, the huge medieval suit of armor on the porch stands as a silent reminder that visitors should be ready for anything, especially ghostly activity.

The Castle Inn stands on land that was once part of the Livaudais Plantation. In 1848, a London-style townhouse was constructed in the 1500 block of Fourth Street. It was the home of a prominent civic leader who was also an organizer of a secret group called the White Man's League, a forerunner of the Ku Klux Klan. After his death, the house was destroyed and the land remained vacant for nearly 40 years.

In 1891, the house now known as the Castle Inn was constructed. It boasts 13-foot-high ceilings, magnificent hardwood floors, fancy moldings, a dramatic staircase, and period antiques that create a feeling that you've traveled back in time to the Big Easy of the 19th century. For some reason, the sinister portrait of the land's former owner, the white supremacist civic leader, still hangs in the hall over the stairs, glaring at guests. Added to all of that, the place is really haunted. The inn proudly displays a certificate from North Florida Paranormal Research, Inc., affirming that "witnessed and documented paranormal events" have occurred here.

Guests of the inn have filled books with their impressions and experiences tied to the presence of two ghosts. You can view these reports on the inn's Web site. The most frequently sighted ghost is that of a charming black man who worked in the mansion as a paid servant and lived in quarters located across the yard. He spoke several languages, was known as a drinker and joker, and was fond of female companionship. He also smoked cigars and cigarettes. One night, after drinking a large quantity of brandy, he fell asleep in his bed before extinguishing his cigar. The resulting smoke was so thick that he died of suffocation. The man apparently enjoyed the mansion and the social benefits of his job so much that he stayed on after his death. In fact, he has moved into the main house, shunning the tight quarters he knew as a servant.

The other ghost at this location is that of a little girl named Emily, also known as Dee. It is believed that she died by falling into a pond when the property was still part of the Livaudais Plantation. Death brought confusion for this little girl because she wanders about looking for her mother. In fact, she has been spotted in several houses in the neighborhood and on the sidewalks as well.

Guests have experienced ghost activity in every room of the inn, including the hallway, staircase, and sitting rooms. Several pages of reports list sounds of knocking on doors, floors, and ceilings; rattling of doorknobs; coughing; singing; speaking in foreign languages; doors slamming; tapping on windows; snoring; heavy footsteps; light running of a child in the hall; furniture being moved; and creaking floor boards. Also, disembodied voices have been heard. An unseen little girl is said to ask guests if they have seen her mother. Her giggling has been heard as well. Some guests have been aroused from sleep by their shaking beds. Others report the feeling that someone is bouncing up and down on the bed or trying to slip under the covers with them.

The male ghost continues his jokes by moving objects. He may arrange shoes in odd patterns, move suitcases, or hide keys, wallets, tickets, or cameras. After futile searches, some guests have found their missing keys mysteriously stashed in the microwave. The inn's ghosts play with light switches and radio and TV controls. One woman ran from her room complaining that the ceiling fan would not shut off. She was astonished when the staff explained that the fan had been disconnected for three years.

Some people have detected the odors of flowers, oranges, and tobacco in several rooms of this non-smoking establishment. Sometimes these odors are noticed moments before the ghosts make contact. Guests have felt someone kiss their cheeks, touch their faces with a soft hand, or stroke their forearms as they lay in bed. Several guests, visiting ghost hunters, and staff have seen apparitions on the stairs and in the guest rooms. A large dark shadow moving about the room during the night is a common experience. Little Emily has been seen on the second floor near the stairs and in the main floor foyer.

There may be other ghosts at this popular Garden District inn. A brave couple who honeymooned there brought along a Ouija board and contacted a spirit named Henry. This spirit claimed he was born in 1854 and died at the age of 39. He did not say if he died in the house or nearby, but his favorite room is number eight. The man was a card player and left several children under the care of his widowed wife. Henry creates light anomalies, such as orbs and clouds, which show up in film and digital photographs.

The Castle Inn has several ghosts and documents that describe the paranormal experiences of its guests.

CAPTIVE SOLDIERS

Griffon House
1447 Constance Street (at Terpsichore Street)
New Orleans 70130-4147

Adam Griffon built this tall, three-story house in 1852. His imposing structure was the finest house in the neighborhood, boasting 14-foot-high ceilings and spacious rooms perfect for fancy balls and other important social events. Griffon lived in the house only ten years before abandoning it in 1862, days before the Union army began its occupation of New Orleans. As Griffon anticipated, his house was commandeered by Union officers and used as a barracks, warehouse, and jail for unruly soldiers. Two of the events that occurred in this house may account for the paranormal activity that many people have experienced here.

When Union soldiers swept through the neighborhood, they stopped at any home that looked prosperous and large enough to accommodate troops, especially high-ranking officers. When soldiers first entered the Griffon House, it is reported that they heard screams, moans, and rattling chains coming from the third floor. When they investigated, they found several slaves chained to the walls, almost dead from starvation and infected wounds. Many of them had wounds from harsh treatment or bizarre experiments. This grisly discovery made it clear that Griffon's escape from New Orleans was prompted by his fear that the mistreatment of his slaves would be discovered instead of the suspected notion that he despised the Yankee invaders. Most of the slaves died soon after removal to a Union army field hospital. It is said that some died as they were carried downstairs.

The misery of the slaves' torture, confinement, and slow, agonizing deaths left strong environmental imprints behind that have been experienced by occupants of the house over the next century. The ghosts of some of these unfortunate people may be here, too, seeking revenge on Adam Griffon.

More frequent hauntings are attributed to two Confederate soldiers who committed a double suicide on the third floor. They were caught looting while wearing Union uniforms. Thinking they might escape severe punishment if they kept up the masquerade, the men were incarcerated in the Griffon House to await the arrival of a senior officer who would act on their case. During their stay, guards informed them that orders had been issued stipulating that any soldier—Union or Confederate—caught looting was to be shot. Realizing their fate was sealed, the men bribed a guard to bring them a bottle of whiskey and two pistols. During their final hour, the men got drunk and sang their favorite songs, filling the attic with their revelry. When the bottle was empty, they reclined on the bed and shot each other in the chest. It is said they bled so much, their blood dripped through the floorboards to the room below.

Reports of strange occurrences in the house started to accumulate in the 1920s. A man who operated a small repair shop in the rear of the house disappeared without a trace. His friends in the neighborhood reported that he was disturbed by strange things he had seen in the house. When pressed for details, he always refused to say anything more.

Occupants of the house in the 1930s reported loud sounds of marching boots. One pair would stomp into a room followed by a second pair. Sometimes startled witnesses heard disembodied singing and boisterous laughing. Later, a second-floor renter reported blood dripping from the ceiling. She also heard ghostly singing and laughter.

For decades, people passing by the Griffon House have spotted the faces of two men in the third-floor attic window. They appear to be dressed in blue uniforms. Others, including ghost hunters, report hearing loud voices singing Civil War-era songs. The most common one was "John Brown's Body."

In May 2005, the Griffon House underwent a major renovation. Renovations often awaken ghosts, attract curious spirits, and increase paranormal activity. Although the house is a private residence, ghost hunters might have some success here because the suicide soldiers have been seen from the street as they gaze out the attic window.

POLTERGEIST OF GALLIER HALL

Lafayette Square
545 St. Charles Avenue
New Orleans 70130-3409
504-565-7457

"There is something strange going on in Gallier Hall," the ghost tour guide said. "It's probably poltergeist activity." Following up on this suggestion, I visited Gallier Hall in May 2005 and found that there is, indeed, something strange going on.

Constructed between 1845 and 1850, Gallier Hall was designed by a leading architect of the day, James Gallier Sr. The huge Greek revival building faces Lafayette Square and served as New Orleans City Hall for more than 100 years. At the front of the building stand six Doric columns and a classic Greek facade. On the Lafayette Street side of the building, three sculptured figure—blind Justice, Liberty, and Commerce—stand in testament of Gallier Hall's original purpose. Aside from a century of city government, its spacious halls and massive rooms were the venue for several important events in the Louisiana's political history, especially during the post-Civil War Reconstruction and the political career of Huey Long. Among the famous figures who lay in state here are Confederate president Jefferson Davis and General P. G. T. Beauregard. Contemporary music legends Earl King and Ernie K-Doe were also accorded that honor.

Gallier Hall consists of three floors, each with wide halls, doorways, and large rooms with high ceilings. Each room can accommodate between 100 and 200 people, depending on the occasion. Today, Gallier Hall is used for meetings, special civic events, and wedding receptions. The third floor of the building is rarely used, and when questioned about this, people who work there refuse to report specific paranormal activity. Speaking on the condition of anonymity, two people who work in the building told me that poltergeist activity is frequent at times and that meetings have been disrupted.

In the spring of 2005, I was permitted access to all floors. A small number of workers moved about the first two floors, some moving

The third floor of Gallier Hall has been the site of poltergeist activity.

furniture while others made preparations for an upcoming event. The third floor was empty and quiet. Passing through the large rooms, I noted no unusual activity. In the men's room, however, something very strange happened.

A door to one of the toilet stalls opened and closed four times in rapid succession. Each time, the door closed gently, without the slamming motion that is often a characteristic of a poltergeist. After viewing this phenomenon, I left the room, saying to myself, "Well, that's not too bizarre." As the door to the restroom closed, there was a loud crash, as if someone had kicked a metal trash bin with a heavy boot. I checked the room immediately, but found no one hiding in the room. The noises stopped, too.

There is no information available through published histories or New Orleans ghost stories that points to the possible identity of the entity in the men's restroom. The paranormal activity may be the work of a ghost. However, if the activity is attributed to a poltergeist, by contemporary definition, the culprit is a living soul who releases emotional energy that acts on the environment.

CHAPTER 3

The French Quarter—
West of Orleans Avenue

Eclectic and fascinating, the historic French Quarter is one of the oldest neighborhoods in America. Writer Joshua Clark proclaimed it the oldest bohemia in the country, boasting more than 200 bars and world-renowned jazz clubs, signature restaurants, and a palpable history that fills its narrow streets like a winter fog. The multiplicity of ethnic groups and cultures, layered and often intermingled, and a history that includes ten wars and six flags raised over Jackson Square, places the Quarter beyond description. Yet, it is accurate to say that the French Quarter is an amazing amalgam—of everything sweet, grand, comedic, and tragic—that attracts ten million visitors each year, capturing the imagination of most of them while seducing many with an intoxicating essence of the place.

The land on which the old quarter—or Vieux Carré—stands was claimed for the king of France by explorers in 1682. Less than 20 years later, Pierre and Jean-Baptiste Le Moyne sailed up the Mississippi River from the Caribbean and landed at place where the river had created a bit of high ground amid swamps and bayous. Making landfall the day before Fat Tuesday, they named the spot Pointe du Mardi Gras.

By the early 1700s, plans for development of the site were underway, headed by John Law and his New Company of the Indies, backed by French financiers. In 1718, a town was established at Pointe du Mardi Gras, on an Indian trail connecting the Mississippi River and Lake Pontchartrain. Within two years, immigrants from France began to arrive. As a tribute to a financial and political supporter of the enterprise, Regent Duc d'Orleans, the town was named La Nouvelle-Orléans.

Dedicated to the notion that the town should embody European traditions and style, the region's first governor, Jean-Baptiste Le Moyne, Sieur de Bienville, commissioned engineer Adrien de Pauger to lay out a grid of 66 blocks. Adrien de Pauger's design included a large public square—later named Jackson Square—at the shores of the Mississippi, designed to impress new arrivals and serve as a point of embarkation for passengers and cargo. La Nouvelle-Orléans quickly filled with immigrants who constructed houses of wood. Most of these burned in the great fire of March 21, 1788. When the city was rebuilt, many improvements were made, including street lights, drainage canals, and codes that required buildings to be constructed of masonry or stone or covered with stucco as well as capped with tile roofs. This farsighted building code contributed to the preservation of hundreds of French Quarter buildings, enabling them to withstand the great fire of 1794 and the destructive hurricanes of 1793, 1794, 1965, and 2005.

In 1762, New Orleans was deeded to Spain in a secret treaty that relieved the French of a colony that had taxed its resources for years. Citizens of the town staged a revolt and refused to relinquish their French identity and allegiance. However, Spanish governance brought many cultural and civic improvements and increased trade with Europe and South America, adding much to the wealth of the lower Mississippi plantations. In 1800, the secret Treaty of San Ildefonso returned the colony to France. Celebrations throughout the French Quarter and Mississippi River plantations had hardly abated when documents were signed in the Cabildo, on Jackson Square, concluding the Louisiana Purchase of 1803 that made the French and Spanish residents American citizens.

In spite of wars, epidemics, several natural disasters, and major changes in governing political institutions, New Orleans has succeeded in developing a unique identity that has endured for nearly three centuries. This has been due, in large part, to an amazing social and cultural flexibility created by blending immigrants from Europe, the Caribbean, northern American states, Canada, South America, and Africa. Today, New Orleans offers a rich culture of food, music, art, dance, theater, architecture, and social history that is unlike any other American city. Even the ghostly atmosphere is unique. Fascinating history is found on dimly lit, narrow streets and glimpsed through wrought-iron gates that hide secret courtyards, alleyways, and cemeteries. Centuries-old buildings that are now popular inns and restaurants beckon the ghost hunter to enjoy a marvelous, vibrant city where even the dead are lively.

THE DEAD SOLDIER

The Cabildo
701 Chartres Street
New Orleans 70116
504-568-6968

This massive building has been standing since 1795 and looks as though it will last forever. It has withstood hurricanes and other disasters, including a fire that gutted the building in 1988. When the Cabildo was completed in 1797, it was the seat of the colonial Spanish government known as the "Illustrious Cabildo." For more than two centuries, it served the people of New Orleans as a center for government agencies before being remodeled as part of the Louisiana State Museum. During the Civil War, officers of the Union army used the building as barracks, offices, and a warehouse. During the War of 1812, a portion of the Cabildo was briefly used as a prison. One of the unfortunate soldiers incarcerated there still haunts the place.

During the War of 1812, the rooms at the rear of the Cabildo, resembling slave quarters, were used to jail British sympathizers suspected of spying on the American army as well as soldiers who failed to do their duties. One young fellow was hastily tried by a military tribunal, found guilty, and hung in the courtyard. Now, the ghost of the dead soldier runs through the building, often creating quite a disturbance. Many visitors have detected a strange presence in several areas of the Cabildo, particularly the hallways of the second floor. In the courtyard, sensitive people may feel pain and sadness at the place where the gallows stood. Some ghost hunters claim to have seen the partial apparition of this young soldier swinging at the end of a rope.

Paranormal activity in the Cabildo increased significantly after renovations following the 1988 fire. The building's security staff have reported sensations of being pushed by invisible hands as they patrol the hallways and stairs. To this day, people who attend social functions at the Cabildo tell of feeling someone rush by them. As the ghost passes, he causes drinks to be spilled and plates of food to be dropped. People who have experienced this describe the perpetrator as a young man. Some see him in a ragged uniform. Security staff members have given up chasing after the rude ghost. The greatest number of sightings seems to be in the courtyard early in the morning. This young soldier was probably executed at sunrise.

FAULKNER'S PIPE

Faulkner House Books
624 Pirate's Alley
New Orleans 70116
504-524-2940

This bookstore is a treasure trove of great literature. The 1840 building is crowded with classic works by authors such as Herman Melville, Ernest Hemingway, John Steinbeck, Frances Parkinson Keyes, and of course, William Faulkner. Newer contributions to the literary legacy of the South can be found, too. Among these is Joshua Clark's collection of French Quarter fiction. The charm of the place goes beyond the fascinating stacks of books, though. As the name implies, Faulkner spent time in this building.

Born in Oxford, Mississippi, in 1897, Faulkner came to New Orleans after the end of World War I. With a formal education that stopped at the tenth grade, but a passion for poetry and prose, Faulkner set up shop in the charming, old building on Pirate's Alley. He was determined to make a go of it as a writer, knowing that poverty and a life exiled to an intellectual wasteland would be his if he failed.

During the day, Faulkner worked at odd jobs for people in the neighborhood. At night, he sat at his desk on the ground floor and created his first book of poems, *The Marble Faun,* published in 1924, and his first novel, *Soldiers' Pay.* As he worked, Faulkner puffed on his pipe, often gaining inspiration from the trail of smoke as it spiraled upward, filling the still air.

Faulkner lived in the French Quarter for only a few years, but he loved the creative atmosphere he found there. Memories of the rhythms of the street and winds off the river stayed with him wherever he traveled. There is some evidence that after his death in 1962, Faulkner returned to the cherished place where he continued writing.

The odor of Faulkner's pipe smoke has been detected on the first floor of the Pirate's Alley bookstore. Visitors and staff milling about the confines of the store encounter the pungent fragrance at the rear of the room and in a small hallway to the right of the store's entrance.

The building at 624 Pirate's Alley is said to date from the 1840s, but a recent visit by a sensitive ghost hunter uncovered the essence of an earlier age. The brick floor, constructed in a herringbone pattern, is believed to be a remnant from an 18th-century structure. While touching the floor, the ghost hunter detected the rapid-paced movement of little feet. Faulkner may be sharing his cherished writing den with other spirits.

LITTLE GIRL AT THE TALL MANSION

626 Pirate's Alley
New Orleans 70116

The upper floors of the magnificent red mansion that sits next to Faulkner House Books offer rare views of St. Anthony's Garden. Looking at the tall house from Pere Antoine Alley, at the far side of the garden, it is easy to imagine relaxing days when occupants of the house would gaze out the windows, secure from the traffic, noise, and odd characters that roamed the nearby streets. They might have felt protected from the frequent epidemics that swept through New Orleans as well. But strong doors and windows, or tall houses that rose above the dirty streets, did little to keep yellow fever or cholera from ravaging even the wealthiest families.

During one of the epidemics of the 1850s, a little girl, eight or nine years old, became ill. Wrapped in blankets and propped up on a chaise in front of a third-floor window, she suffered through her

The ghost of a little girl who died of yellow fever has been seen in the third-floor window of this Pirate's Alley mansion.

fevers, longing to return to play with her friends in St. Anthony's Garden. As she grew weaker, her only wish became stronger. Even after her death, the little girl is said to still sit by the third-floor window gazing at the gardens. From Pere Antoine Alley, ghost hunters see her face pressed to the glass. Her white gown and long, brown hair are seen, too. The ghostly image does not move but there are reports that she sometimes appears in a fourth-floor window.

A recent tour of the house, granted by one of its residents, did not turn up any ghosts. But, near a third-floor window over looking St. Anthony's Garden, I detected a sensation of great sadness. Sunlight, scattered by the tall, old window, hardly penetrated the room. Within a foot or two of the windows, the place seemed filled with shadows, leaving the impression that some kind of environmental imprint, created by profound sadness and, perhaps, the unfulfilled wish of a little girl, has remained for more than 150 years. Little is known of her short life. We do know that she was one of thousands of children who died in New Orleans from infectious diseases, congenital defects, malnutrition, and injuries, which today are easily cured. In spite of her illness, she left behind something that tells us about her dreams, something of great strength.

GHOSTS OF THE MURDERED MISTRESS AND BETRAYED WIFE

Former site of Royal Café
700 Royal Street
New Orleans 70116

Jean Baptiste LaBranche was an accomplished practitioner of the old New Orleans tradition known as plaçage. Plaçage was an arrangement by which wealthy, married, white gentlemen kept mistresses who were usually *demoiselles de couleur,* or free young ladies of color. These liaisons often lasted years and provided the philandering husbands with comforts and freedoms that were somehow absent from their legal marriages. LaBranche's wife, the demure Marie Melanie Trepagnier, apparently knew nothing of the arrangement although plaçage was widely practiced in the 18th and early 19th centuries.

French Quarter gentlemen never spoke openly about these secret liaisons, and they covered for each other, when necessary, maintaining confidences that, if divulged, could ruin a man.

LaBranche maintained his family in a huge house built in 1796 on the corner of Royal and St. Peter streets. He enjoyed his luxurious home and the pleasures of his mistress, whom he kept in a small cottage in the upper quarter until the day he died in 1842. It is said that two gentlemen who attended LaBranche's funeral made comments about his mistress, Melissa, within earshot of the grieving widow. Following a few leads, Marie discovered the name of her husband's mistress and invited her to the Royal Street mansion for tea. The invitation was unusual, at the very least, but the young woman accepted. Once inside the house, Marie assaulted Melissa, tied her up, and dragged her to the attic. There, the poor woman was chained to the wall and starved to death.

The most photographed building in the French Quarter houses the former Royal Café and the ghosts of two women.

Somehow, Marie LaBranche managed to reside in the house while her prisoner suffered a slow death. In fact, Marie remained there until her death in 1858. The horrendous act of murder—the slow death inflicted by a betrayed and vengeful wife—has trapped the ghosts of these women together in the same house. The ghost of the mistress, Melissa, is quite active in the mansion that for many years housed the Royal Café. She makes appearances on the second and third floors, moving tables and chairs to positions of her liking, and sometimes throwing cups and glasses across the room. This ghost generates a sense of anger or restlessness for sensitive visitors.

Marie LaBranche also haunts the second floor. She has been seen wearing a blue dress with long hair cascading down her back. Former restaurant staff and patrons could detect when the murderer was present; she creates an atmosphere of tension as if some strong authority is conducting an inspection. Indeed, this matron of the mansion looks over the living souls as they enjoy the cuisine and hospitality of Royal Café. Many feel as though someone is standing behind them, looking over their shoulder at their food and drinks.

Ghost hunters have encountered cold spots in several places in this old building. Staff tell of lights that go on and off, doors that slam shut, and objects that are mysteriously displaced. If you want to get the attention of Marie or the mistress, go to the second floor and talk about Jean Baptiste, his betrayed wife, and his murdered mistress.

LE PETIT THÉÂTRE DU VIEUX CARRÉ

616 St. Peter Street
New Orleans 70139
504-522-9958

There are few certainties in ghost hunting. But when it comes to haunted places, ships and theaters offer ghost hunters the greatest opportunities for encounters with the spirit world. Theaters often harbor the ghosts of actors, writers, musicians, and directors because something about their creative natures ties them to the place where they experienced their greatest successes or failures. Stagehands and other production staff may haunt backstage areas where they worked and, perhaps, suffered a fatal accident. They may also be tied to rooms where props are stored. The ghosts of patrons remain long after death because they love the theater or, more likely, they love an actor who performed regularly at the location. Le Petit Théâtre du Vieux Carré has several ghosts of actors, stagehands, and patrons in addition to a group of children who also roam about Crescent City Books on Chartres Street.

Le Petit Théâtre opened in 1922 and has been presenting plays, recitals, and musicals for French Quarter residents and visitors for nearly 85 years. The facility is actually two theaters—a small one for children's productions and another with a large stage and seating for hundreds of patrons. A spacious lobby serves both and offers easy access to a large courtyard.

The original corner building, at Chartres and St. Peter streets, was designed by Gilberto Guillemard for Baptiste Orso, a wealthy member of high society. Construction was completed in 1794, but the building was destroyed the same year in the great fire. In 1797, reconstruction was completed and the building became the residence of the last Spanish governor of the colony, Don Manuel Gayoso de Lemos. This portion of the complex now houses the small theater and a portion of the lobby. The large theater, dressing rooms, and offices were constructed in 1922 after the removal of three small buildings that faced St. Peter Street.

Two actresses died tragically at the theater. In 1926, Katherine was a fledging actress who had demonstrated some talent in small roles. After attracting the interest of a successful director, she made a bid for the lead role in an upcoming production. Much to the surprise of others in the theater company, Katherine won the role. She may have pinned her hopes on something more than her talent as an actress because something soured days before opening night. The director replaced her with a rival actress, throwing Katherine into a deep depression. Seeking revenge and an end to her humiliation and suffering, Katherine climbed to the catwalks over the stage, tied a rope around her neck, and jumped to her death before a packed house. Her misery, and the violent way she chose to end her life, has tied her to Le Petit Théâtre. Patrons, visitors, and theater staff have seen her apparition on the stage and in the attic, crying amid a large collection of costumes. Psychics have detected Katherine's strong emotions. Anger, bitterness, and sorrow have been experienced by sensitive people visiting the stage and exploring the attic. Some sense Katherine's terror as she dropped from the catwalk.

In 1924, 22-year-old Caroline died in the courtyard. Even at a young age, this dedicated actress could not comprehend a life beyond the walls of a theater. But unlike Katherine, this talented woman had starred in several productions and her future on the stage seemed bright. Perhaps to assure her success, she was involved with another actor who had established a great career in the theater. In fact, she was with him one evening, on the balcony overlooking the courtyard, enjoying an amorous encounter before curtain call. Caught up in the moment, Caroline slipped over the balcony and fell to her death.

Caroline often appears dressed in a wedding gown, her costume for the opening scene she was to play the night of her death, but she is good at making quick changes. Many have seen her in various styles of dress and with different hair styles. Theater staff believe Caroline is happy and that she has found a fulfilling role as a ghost who finds lost items. When a specific prop cannot be found in the cluttered storage rooms, staff members call out, "Hey, Caroline, where is it?" A few minutes later, the lost item appears, set apart from everything else. Caroline also creates a sense of ease and tranquility, in addition to a dramatic cold spot.

Caroline's skill at finding elusive and much-needed objects is an essential counter to the tendency of another ghost to hide things. Sigmund, the ghost of a stage carpenter believed to have died at the theater, hides objects, plays jokes on stage crews, and creates confusion whenever possible. Sigmund's apparition has been seen by many in several areas within the theater. Audiences have seen him standing in the wings during many plays and musicals. He is described as a short man with salt-and-pepper hair and muscular arms. His partial apparition has startled ghost hunters and other visitors to the theater. One visitor was shocked to feel and see Sigmund's arm and hand come to rest on her shoulder. At times, only his lower legs and boots appear, walking the dark spaces backstage. A paranormal research group reported an episode in which Sigmund appeared completely lifelike to a young man who was waiting for his girlfriend to finish work in the office. The young man had a lengthy conversion with Sigmund. The ghost was so entertaining that the young man invited Sigmund to dinner!

A group of child spirits has been detected at Le Petit Théâtre by psychics and ghost hunters as well. They are often heard laughing, singing, and moving about in the small theater. Some of them like to play with the phones, fax machines, and computers in the office. One of them, a girl named Stephanie, has been known to sit in the lap of visitors who take a break during a tour and drop into a seat for a brief rest. She likes to snuggle and rest her head on the comforting chest of adults. How Stephanie came to haunt the theater is unknown. It has been reported that she was abducted, then raped and murdered under a New Orleans bridge. Somehow, she joined a group of ghost children who wander back and forth between the Crescent City Bookstore at 203 Chartres and Le Petit Théâtre.

Ghosts of former actors and children roam the historic Le Petit Théâtre du Vieux Carré.

Not all the spirits at this location are playful and friendly. Ghost investigators have discovered a malevolent spirit named Perry. He often manifests as a dark shadow or cloud that blocks doors, hallways, or stairways. Perry also makes intense cold spots and strange noises that witnesses are unable to describe. His shirtless apparition has been seen standing on the vacant stage, shaking his fist, and yelling at anybody who comes near. Some people believe that Perry was a slave who died in the oldest part of the theater complex.

Virtually every theater has at least one patron who develops a crush on an actress but keeps his feelings secret. Most of these people foolishly believe their frequent appearances at the theater won't give away their infatuation, but Alejandro Venegas doesn't hide his love for the stage, or any actress who appears on it. He takes his regular balcony seat—second seat from the right aisle, front row—for nearly every performance. The gentleman appears to be an elderly Spaniard with thick black hair and a mustache. Dressed in formal wear from the early 1800s, this ghost appears so lifelike that people holding a ticket for his seat have returned to the box office demanding that the gentleman be removed. Theater staff just smile and assure the patron that if they return to the seat, they will find the gentleman gone.

One writer of ghost stories described Señor Venegas—called the Captain in some accounts—as being a frequent patron of the theater who died before he could reveal his love for a young actress. The man's style of dress, though, is more than 100 years out of date. It is possible that Venegas died in the building when it was the residence of the Spanish governor and more than a century later fell in love with a 1920s actress.

Ghost hunters may want to make several visits to this charming and historic theater. During daylight hours, visit the courtyard where Caroline died and the lobby with its floor made of ballast stones. Ask theater staff about guided tours to backstage areas, dressing rooms, and prop storage rooms. They may allow you to leave a recorder in these areas for an hour or two in order to capture electronic voice phenomena. You should also attend an evening performance. Purchase tickets for a balcony seat and arrive early to get a glimpse of the ghostly Señor Venegas.

GHOSTS OF THE MISTRESS, MURDERER, AND WIDOW

Former site of O'Flaherty's Irish Channel Pub
508 Toulouse Street
New Orleans 70130

In the early 1990s, O'Flaherty's Irish Channel Pub was considered one of the most haunted places in the French Quarter. Psychics and ghost hunters, using various instruments such as electromagnetic field detectors and electronic thermometers, have gathered considerable evidence that three ghosts with close ties haunt this place. After a number of years of amazing encounters with ghosts, the International Society for Paranormal Investigations announced that the building was no longer haunted. Clairvoyants associated with the ISPR claimed to have performed a remote cleansing of the pub, freeing the entities to move on. Confident that off-site, psychic intervention can dissolve a spirit's attachment to a specific building, the ISPR removed O'Flaherty's Irish Channel Pub from its list of Ghost Expeditions' haunted properties.

Ghost hunters who don't share ISPR's confidence in remote cleansing of earth-bound entities continue to visit O'Flaherty's. Many of them experience a lot of ghostly activity. The event that led to the haunting by three identified entities is so heinous and miserable that it is no surprise that environmental imprints and spirit remnants persist despite "cleansing" or release rituals.

The three ghosts who inhabit O'Flaherty's are linked by adultery, murder, and suicide. In 1806, Mary Wheaton married her third husband, Joseph Baptandiere (spelled Bapendier in some accounts). They established their residence on the second floor of the building at 508 Toulouse Street and opened a feed store on the ground floor. By 1810, the rotund, oily-faced, balding Joseph developed an infatuation with the demure Angelique DuBois, who worked in the store.

In the early 1800s, New Orleans gentlemen of means often established relationships with free women of color or white Creole women. The practice is known as the plaçage system and offered many mutual benefits that the gentlemen believed outweighed the risks. Following the tradition and common practice, Joseph established a plaçage arrangement with Angelique. These two unlikely

The former O'Flaherty's Irish Channel Pub occupies the site of a murder-suicide.

lovers were involved for only a short time before Angelique demanded that Joseph leave his wife and marry her. The pretty Angelique was a desirable mistress, but Joseph must have believed she would not make a good wife. Added to that, Mary's money, garnered from two previous marriages, probably strengthened Joseph's desire to at least maintain the legalities of his marriage.

One day, quite an argument developed as Joseph listened, once again, to Angelique's insistence that he do away with Mary and become her husband. Angelique ran from Joseph, dashed upstairs to the third floor of the building, possibly seeking the asylum of her small rented room. In a rage, Joseph followed. Panting and sweating, he chased Angelique through the spacious rooms, finally pinning her against the brick wall that faces Toulouse Street. Angelique must have pressed her demands or, as many storytellers put it, threatened to tell Mary of Joseph's infidelity, because he grabbed her throat and choked her to unconsciousness. Joseph reportedly dragged her nearly lifeless body across the room and threw her through an open window.

Angelique landed in the courtyard and suffered a broken neck. Within seconds, she was dead. Joseph rushed downstairs to cover up his crime before passersby might see the crumpled body on the bricks that covered the courtyard. He dragged the body across the courtyard and stuffed it into a sewage well. His dirty work was hardly finished when he spotted a teenage boy peeking out a fourth-floor window. It was clear to Joseph that the boy had witnessed the crime, in addition to the argument that led to it. Knowing that a witness, together with the blood stains on the courtyard, would seal his fate, Joseph ran back to the third floor, tied a rope around his neck, and jumped out of a window. His neck snapped, killing him.

Eventually, the truth of Joseph's plaçage arrangement with Angelique was revealed. In spite of the horrible murder-suicide and the adultery that took place in her own house, Mary continued to live on the second floor of the building and operate the feed store until her death in March 1817 at age 35.

Today, the ghosts of Mary, Joseph, and Angelique have been encountered at locations within the Toulouse Street building at which the murder-suicide and Mary's final lonely years took place. For many years, visitors and ghost hunters felt a large, intense cold spot in the courtyard over a raised brick planter. According to legend, Joseph dumped Angelique's body into a sewage well that was located there. Sensitive visitors still feel dramatic temperature changes as they pass a hand over the planter, site of the ignominious grave. Angelique's apparition has been seen in the courtyard wandering among participants of ghost tours. Many claim to have seen her and offer similar descriptions. She appears to be thin, of medium height, and in her early 20s. Her brown hair hangs straight, almost reaching her waist. Angelique is said to like young men and children, often touching their hands.

The ghost of Joseph Baptandiere also appears in the courtyard. His restless specter creates unrest among ghost hunters, sometimes leaving scratch marks or depressions in the flesh of their arms. His presence also creates friction among visitors, giving rise to sudden arguments and belligerent attitudes. The International Society for Paranormal Research reports that members of its ghost tours have been assaulted by Joseph in the balcony overlooking Danny O'Flaherty's Ballad Room. One woman was thrown to the ground, almost losing consciousness. Others have been pushed about by a presence they perceive as a tall fat man. Joseph may be responsible for the paranormal activity observed in the Celtic Gift Shop that stands across the courtyard.

The long-suffering Mary Wheaton Baptandiere has remained in the building for nearly 200 years, tied here by tragedy, betrayal, and years of loneliness that followed Angelique's murder. Mary looks after things in the bar and restaurant, often letting new staff members know of her disapproval if they fail to measure up to O'Flaherty's standards. Mary's favorite spot seems to be the balcony overlooking the Ballad Room. While Danny O'Flaherty sings his Irish songs, audiences have been drawn to the apparition of a woman sitting alone. Mary's ghost can be seen from the courtyard in a second-floor window overlooking the spot where Angelique died.

Ghost hunters also believe the ghosts of yellow fever victims inhabit the building. During the epidemic of 1853, the third floor—and possibly the second and fourth floors—was used to quarantine the terminally ill. Most who were sequestered there died. The final phase of the illness was so protracted that several people tried to jump from the windows, ending their misery on the courtyard bricks. Iron bars were installed on the windows to stop such suicide attempts.

The iron bars that imprisoned victims of yellow fever are visible from the court-yard of O'Flaherty's Irish Channel Pub.

I viewed the large room on the third floor in May 2005. Worn brick around the two fireplaces, original 1790 heavy-plank flooring, and filtered light through dust-covered windows contributed to the strange atmosphere. I found cold spots at several locations in the large room, predominantly by the fireplaces. There was also an atmosphere of sadness, fear, and hopelessness. Near the windows, the atmosphere thickened as if some unseen force prevented an easy approach. At times, when street noise was minimal, muted coughing and sniffing could be heard.

O'Flaherty's Irish Channel Pub, though no longer open to the public, is still haunted. Ghost hunters who devote the necessary time to their preparation and investigation may experience some of the French Quarter's most active ghosts.

Other Irish pubs in the French Quarter may house restless spirits that do not come in a bottle. The best time to visit these popular watering holes is in the morning when the doors first open. Virtually every day of the week, late afternoon and evening crowds create a jovial atmosphere that will make ghost hunting difficult.

Kerry's Irish Pub

331 Decatur Street
New Orleans 70130
504-527-5954

Intense cold spots have been encountered here even on very warm nights.

Flanagan's Pub

626 St. Philip Street
New Orleans 70116
504-598-9002

A number of ghost tours meet at this pub. (See Appendix D.) Ghost hunters have encountered the ghost of Angela in the women's restroom and other spots in this cozy pub. Stories suggest that Angela, a longtime regular at the bar and sister of a former owner, committed suicide in the ladies' room.

Ryan's Irish Pub

241 Decatur Street
New Orleans 70130
504-523-3500

The apparition of a bewildered black man shows up here surprising people who sit near the back wall. Dressed in workman's clothes, this ghost may be that of a warehouseman who died in the great fire that swept through this neighborhood.

THE HANDS OF SLAVES

Old Slave Quarters, The Keuffers Building
Corner of Chartres and Toulouse streets
New Orleans 70130

At the corner of Chartres and Toulouse streets stands an old building known as the Keuffers. The upper floors have stood empty for many years while various businesses have tried to make a go of it on the ground floor. The last business was a typical French Quarter drinking establishment that, contrary to tradition, closed not too long after opening. In the spring of 2005, the building and the slave quarters that stand behind it underwent major renovation.

The apparition of a young, white female has been seen at the second-floor windows that face Toulouse Street. She stares at street traffic, occasionally moving the old shudders that hang inside the windows. It will be interesting to see if ghostly activity here becomes more frequent once the renovations are completed.

The slave quarters behind Keuffers are visited by almost every ghost tour in town. Ghost hunters and curious tourists who visit this site are told a sad story of several slave children who were confined

Tall, narrow structures that served as slave quarters can be spotted at several locations in the French Quarter. This building, behind the Keuffers, was used to quarantine yellow-fever victims.

there during the yellow fever epidemic of 1853. Psychics and other sensitive people have seen their anguished faces in the windows facing Toulouse Street. Those who see the children clearly report that they are crying and reaching out to passersby. Some witnesses also report the apparition of a tall black man pacing the second- and third-floor balconies with a whip in his hand.

Behind the building, a sheer wall rises three stories above a modern parking lot broken only by small windows about one foot square. There is no glass in these windows, only iron bars that confined sick slave children who might have tried to squirm through the openings to escape the dark, hot rooms of the building and avoid the cries of others who were dying. Ghost hunters who place their hands through these openings often feel the touch of the slave children. The ISPR estimates that about 30 percent of the people who do this experience some sort of ghostly phenomena. Some people sense the fear and sadness of the sick children who were imprisoned here.

Ghost hunters who put their hands through this barred window behind the Keuffers might feel the touch of the sick children who were confined there.

Upon reaching far into the darkened room, I saw the apparition of a small black hand passing through my outstretched hand. A change in temperature was also noted, but it was impossible to dismiss the influence of local environmental factors.

NEW ORLEANS PHARMACY MUSEUM

514 Chartres Street
New Orleans 70130
504-565-8028

Dr. Louis J. Duffulo, a physician and the first registered pharmacist in the United States, built this apothecary and townhouse in 1823 and practiced his profession here for nearly 35 years. Upon his death, Dr. Dupas purchased the building. Soon after Dupas opened his practice, the apothecary and clinic lost its reputation as a place of compassion and healing. Mysterious things began to happen; people entered the building never to be seen again.

This was the result of Dr. Dupas' fascination with experimental pharmacology and his lack of ethics. On the second floor, he conducted experiments on pregnant slaves and others with ailments that escaped diagnosis. He concocted potions that combined voodoo ingredients, ancient herbal remedies, and the latest medicines from Europe. These substances were given in large doses without regard to side effects. Indeed, many of the doctor's patients succumbed without evidence that the initial illness was favorably affected. Treatments given to female slaves resulted in terrible birth defects and often the death of the mothers.

There is reason to believe that Dr. Dupas secretly disposed of the bodies by passing them through a second-floor trap door into a wagon waiting in the carriageway on the left side of the building. Psychic investigators have sensed that bodies for experimentation were also brought into the building by this secret route. Sensitive people standing at this location feel nauseated while experiencing a profound sadness.

Dr. Dupas carried on his heinous experiments until his death, but he has not left the building. The staff of the pharmacy museum, visitors, and ghost hunters have seen a distinguished-looking man in a brown suit and white lab coat. He is described as short and stocky, about 65 years old, with a mustache. Dr. Dupas appears on the first and second floors of the building. He moves around the shop, checking cabinets, medicine bottles, and instruments, and sometimes moves objects inside locked cases.

Psychics claim that he creates such negative energy that sensitive people have strong physical reactions even if they are standing outside the building. When the evil doctor is present, pregnant women are particularly prone to feel nauseated, short of breath, and to experience abdominal pain. Reactions such as these also occur in the second-floor chamber that contains a large bed and a collection of medical instruments, including devices for drawing blood and assisting with childbirth. Ghost hunters have also detected a female entity in the courtyard by the fountain. This spot is surrounded by a medicinal herb garden established by Dr. Dupas. The ISPR estimates the frequency for experiencing paranormal phenomena at the New Orleans Pharmacy Museum may be as high as 40 percent.

NAPOLEON HOUSE

500 Chartres Street
New Orleans 70130
504-524-9752

Mayor Nicholas Girod built this huge house in 1814 with a spacious courtyard, balconies, and a cupola similar to those on the roofs of the Cabildo and Presbytere. He was so proud of his grand mansion that, while hosting a party in 1821, he offered the place to the imprisoned emperor Napoleon of France should he escape from Elba Island and seek asylum in America. There was little chance the emperor would take him up on the offer, but Girod, being a skilled politician, gained political mileage from the magnanimous gesture. From that point on, the citizens of New Orleans referred to the mansion as the Napoleon House.

Today, the Napoleon House is a busy restaurant serving locals and tourists in an open-air bar, in-house dining room, and courtyard setting. The place is typically busy any day of the week from the

Mayor Nicholas Girod built his house in 1814 and offered it as asylum to Napoleon. Today, it is the site of the Napoleon House bar and restaurant.

moment doors open until they close. The rustic walls, nearly 200 years old, are filled with portraits of Napoleon and panoramas of his battles. The lone departure from this imperial French theme is the portrait of Pete Impastato, who owned the restaurant from 1936 to 1971. Over the two centuries of its existence, the building has served as home to several families.

During the Civil War, wounded soldiers, Confederate and Union, were treated at an infirmary on the second floor. With limited medical care, many soldiers died here. When shadows fall across the balcony that overlooks Chartres Street, a soldier in a gray uniform can be seen. He walks half its length and then disappears. Patient ghost hunters have seen him reappear within a few minutes to begin the walk again. Sometimes he is seen leaning on the balcony oblivious to modern traffic below.

In the courtyard, the apparition of a black woman appears dressed in long skirts with a bandana tied around her head. This ghost has been described as a "mammy," traditionally a slave governess, head of a large kitchen staff, or nursemaid. It is likely that the courtyard was her place of death or had something to do with her household duties, such as the supervision of children there. Paranormal investigators believe that renovations made in the 1990s upset the mammy. During that time, sensitive visitors noted that the atmosphere in the bar and restaurant was heavy and oppressive. Bartenders saw bottles knocked over, spilling expensive liquor. Mammy must have approved of the renovations, however. When they were completed, things got back to normal, and she took up her usual place in the courtyard.

CRESCENT CITY BOOKS

204 Chartres Street
New Orleans 70130
504-524-4997

Property records for this location date back to 1808, when the block was sold with several existing buildings. Local historians believe other structures stood there but they were destroyed in the fires of 1788 and 1794. In 1829, Louis Pecquet purchased the land, cleared it of existing buildings, and constructed a large commercial building. In 1870, the land changed hands once again. Pecquet's building was torn down and replaced with a new structure that now houses Crescent City Books.

On the first two floors, this charming, cluttered bookstore contains thousands of rare books that captivate readers and browsers for hours. Large over-stuffed chairs provide a comfortable place for visitors to leaf through fascinating texts—fiction, poetry, and nonfiction. In this bookstore, the living are quiet. The dead are making the noise.

On the first floor, to the right, a child named Christopher haunts the bookshelves. He wanders about, touching the books and occasionally pulling them off the shelves. On the second floor, people have detected several children. They climb over the overstuffed chairs, moving the cushions and pushing books to the floor. Sometimes, their laughter is heard as they rush from the large windows facing the street to the rear of the floor and down the stairs.

Ghosts of children play on the second and third floors of Crescent City Books. The little ghosts also appear down the street at Le Petit Théâtre du Vieux Carré.

In the mid-1990s, a psychic investigation revealed a male presence on the second floor. This fellow, about 27 years old and dressed in clothes typical of the 1880s, was attracted to the rare books in the store. He died elsewhere and had no specific connection with this building or location in the Vieux Carré.

Investigators discovered the ghosts of two murder victims on the third floor. One was a young man who suffered a stab wound. The other was a 20-year-old woman who was killed by forced drug overdose. Both of these unfortunate souls died elsewhere but have found refuge in this quiet, old building. These ghosts generate an atmosphere of sadness. The young man's death was so violent that one psychic investigator tasted blood in her mouth.

In the attic, cold spots and electromagnetic-field changes signal the presence of another entity. This ghost was seen dressed in a fancy suit complete with gold watch and chain, wearing gold-rimmed glasses. Some believe this is Louis Pecquet, who resides in his building, protecting it from yet another fire.

Ghost hunters who attempt to photograph the spirits in Crescent City Books have been frustrated by mechanical failures, electromagnetic interference, and batteries that suddenly go dead. On the second floor, patient ghost hunters may see cushions change their shape as little spirits climb into the big chairs to read a favorite storybook.

MONTELEONE HOTEL

214 Royal Street
New Orleans 70130
510-523-3341

This spectacular four-star hotel, rising high above Royal Street in the Vieux Carré, seems an unlikely place to encounter ghosts. The Monteleone's modern amenities, well-lit hallways, and quiet but busy lobby are at odds with the very old buildings of the Quarter that sit on quiet, dimly lit streets where you might expect to find roaming spirits. But the Monteleone Hotel is haunted.

In recent years, guests and staff have experienced a lot of paranormal activity. During personal introductions among a group embarking on one of the French Quarter's ghost tours, a couple from Chicago introduced themselves to their companions by saying they came for the ghosts and found them at their hotel, the Monteleone. Several times during their five-day stay, they heard the sounds of children playing in the hallways. When they opened the door to investigate, the hallway was empty. At the end of his first day in town, the man placed his shoes next to his bed before heading for the shower. Later, he found a matching earring in each shoe. His wife, a jewelry consultant, estimated their value at well over $100. The earrings were not hers or discarded by a previous occupant, and no visitors had entered their room. The couple believed a ghost placed these expensive bobbles in the shoes. Some spirits are good at relocating objects, even from one room to another. At the world-famous haunted plantation, the Myrtles, in St. Francisville, the ghost, Chloe, is known for her skill at removing one earring from ladies who visit the home. This ghost needs only one earring because her right ear was chopped off as punishment for eavesdropping.

The history of the Monteleone's location is hard to decipher since it sits on a part of the French Quarter where buildings were replaced several times over the past 180 years. Ghostly remnants from previous structures are likely present in the newer building. Their reason for being there, however, is unclear.

It is interesting to note that the Monteleone Hotel does not have a 13th floor. Structurally, the 14th floor is the 13th level above the street. The couples from Chicago detected the ghostly sounds of children at play in the hallway on the 14th floor. Hotel housekeeping staff discreetly admit to frequent encounters with ghostly apparitions on several floors, many of them children.

THE PASS-THROUGH GHOST

Café Beignet
334-B Royal Street
New Orleans 70130
504-523-5530

A few minutes after seven in the morning, this little café is busy

The ghost of a Native American woman may appear at Café Beignet.

with locals and tourists savoring fresh beignets and coffee. Throughout the day, the flow of customers continues for sandwiches and Southern specialties. Few who sit inside the cozy café, surrounded by ancient brick walls and ceiling, notice the pale apparition of a young woman dressed in Native American clothing. She passes from the wall, closest to the courtyard, to the opposite wall, disappearing into the bricks.

The woman's clothing and apparent movement through the brick walls suggests this is a haunting created before the building was erected. For centuries before French explorers claimed the land in 1718, Indians used this ground to pass from the Mississippi River to Lake Pontchartrain. This woman may have spent a great deal of time at this spot, awaiting the return of a husband or son or caring for someone who died here. Repetitive tasks carried out during a period of great emotional stress may have created the environmental imprint. The woman moves slowly, not turning her head or moving her arms. Some believe she is carrying a blanket or animal skin. This apparition is best seen when the café is empty of customers at closing time.

Former employees report that they have had frequent encounters with this ghost late in the evening.

GHOST OF MR. PERCY

Brennan's
417 Royal Street
New Orleans 70130
504-525-9711

The quiet ghost of Mr. Percy is often sensed or seen watching over the elegant crowd as they enjoy a superb dining experience at this world-class restaurant. Mr. Percy appears on the balcony overlooking the courtyard, on the staircase in the entry, and under the tree that shades outdoor diners. His identity is unknown, but his keen interest in the restaurant may be a clue as to who he is and why he remains at this location. Some historians and ghost hunters believe he was a slave who worked on the property as a caretaker. Others dispute this idea and suggest he was a former owner or occupant of the house, a banker, or a waiter.

The first recorded owner of this property was Baron Hambourg, in 1721, whom some people believe is the ghost known as Mr. Percy. On December 3, 1794, the property was sold to Gaspar Debuys and Huberto Remy. Five days later, they watched the trees and structures on their land go up in smoke with the great fire of 1794 that destroyed a major portion of New Orleans. Not long after the fire—on January 8, 1795—Debuys and Remy were able to unload the damaged property. The structure that stands at 417 Royal Street today was built in 1795 by Don Vincente Rillieux. In 1805, the building was sold to Julien Poydras, who opened the Bank of Louisiana. This financial institution thrived until 1820, when the bank was liquidated and the property sold to Martin Gordon. Substantial renovations converted it from a business establishment to a lavish home known for Creole parties and important social events. In 1954, Owen Brennan renovated the building and opened his celebrated restaurant. Fire struck the place again in 1975, but Brennan's was rebuilt and open for business again only six months later.

A long list of French Quarter notables who lived or worked at 417

Royal Street—including chess master Paul Morphy who died in the building—might offer clues as to the identity of the tall, quiet ghost known as Mr. Percy. The pale apparition might be a banker, a slave, a former waiter at Brennan's, or a Creole gentleman who cannot leave the site of so many happy and exciting affairs. Rumors are that the building occupied by Brennan's has a large brick oven that might have been a crematorium. If this place once served as a mortuary, the ghost of Mr. Percy might be that of an undertaker.

Sensitive ghost hunters who dine at Brennan's report a female presence in the courtyard and on the staircase. It has been reported that the ghost of chef Paul Blange has been seen haunting the restaurant he loved so much. Blange created the restaurant's signature dessert, bananas Foster. The ghost of wine master Herman Funk roams about the place, too. He has been spotted in the wine cellar and occasionally shows up at tables when rare vintages are poured.

Other interesting restaurants where ghost hunters may encounter spirits of the dead include:

La Louisiane Restaurant

725 Iberville Street
New Orleans 70116
504-581-7300

Look for the ghost of Mrs. LeDoux. She was known for opening her home to destitute women who faced starvation rather than engage in prostitution.

Muriel's Jackson Square

801 Chartres Street
New Orleans 70116
504-568-1885

Three ghosts may be found here. Pierre Antoine Lepardi Jourdan committed suicide upstairs in 1814. His pale apparition has been seen throughout the restaurant. The other ghosts are believed to be patrons of a bar that operated there for many years. They died in barroom brawls but remain behind, sometimes throwing glasses, tipping bottles, and tapping on windows.

THE SILENT WITNESSES

Louisiana Supreme Court Building
400 Royal Street
New Orleans 70130
504-310-2300

Police officials and the prosecuting attorney promised the witnesses—a young white woman and an older black man—protection. Guards would watch over them, they said. Without their testimony, prosecutors insisted, the criminals would go free. The young woman and the older man were frightened, but they knew they could not live with themselves if they failed to appear in court. They were key witnesses against mafia hit men. They alone could identify the killers and rid New Orleans of a terrible scourge that had corrupted the city and preyed upon its citizens since the 1890s.

As they passed through the large hallways filled with police, reporters, and curious citizens, they started to relax. With so many people around, surely no one could harm them. When they entered the courtroom, a different kind of nervousness took over. Each was to speak before the judge, a jury, attorneys, and the accused. But before the judge could gavel the assembly to order, shots rang out. The witnesses fell to the floor, mortally wounded. The crowd in the courtroom burst into confusion as people dashed for the exits or dove under tables. Some tried to comfort the victims but it was clear they died instantly from large caliber wounds inflicted at close range. Bailiffs scrambled, grabbing suspicious characters who might be the assassins. But this was 1930. Courtroom security was little more than a few aging police with pistols. The bad guys got away while the witnesses, the old man and young woman, lay dead in pools of blood.

These brave souls were so resigned to giving testimony that they

The ghosts of murdered witnesses still haunt the Louisiana Supreme Court Building in the French Quarter.

still roam the hallway of the 1909 courthouse, perhaps waiting to be called to the witness stand. The nearly solid apparitions have been seen in the first-floor hallway. They move from one end of the hallway to the other, vanishing as guards approach.

Another apparition has been spotted on the third floor looking out the window at the Omni Hotel on St. Louis Street. This ghost, seen in a white shirt and tie, is believed to be a lawyer. He might be the prosecutor who lost his key witnesses in the courthouse shooting. Additional entities have been detected on the sidewalks surrounding the marble and granite courthouse. On Chartres Street, ghost hunters with the ISPR felt a woman touch them on their arms. She is perceived to be crying and begs to be allowed to see her children. Others have encountered the pale apparition of a thin man with a thick, dark beard who is lying on the Royal Street sidewalk. Propped against the granite and iron fence, he reaches out as if begging from passersby. This poor fellow probably died at this spot from alcohol or drug abuse.

This magnificent example of federalist architecture stands in sharp contrast with much older French Quarter building styles. Photographic equipment, including cell phones with imaging features, is not permitted inside the building.

ORBS AND CLOUDS

The Court of Two Sisters
613 Royal Street
New Orleans 70130
504-522 7261

The entrance on Royal Street is plain enough, just old, red brick accented with the number 613, and a sign with the name of this famous restaurant. But when you enter the brick-lined passageway leading to the wide doors, everything changes to a mystical quality. Huge iron gates, a gift from Queen Isabella of Spain, stand open as if they are gathering visitors from the modern world and directing them to a place from another time. The gates themselves have a mystical quality, complete with a promise that, "A charm passes to anyone who touches these gates." Many who touch them find a wish granted within ten days.

After passing through the wide doors, the brick ceiling opens, the foyer widens, and visitors get a glimpse of the magical courtyard that lies beyond. To the right, a staircase rises with iron railings. During a May 2005 visit, I detected a male presence on these stairs. I didn't see an apparition, but found a large cold spot on the landing. The male presence may be frightened or concerned by changes to the building or feel threatened by the crowds passing through the foyer.

Moving further into the building, an ancient bar sits to the right. The courtyard comes into view, giving the impression of a Disneyland fantasy, complete with a trademark New Orleans fountain, trees and lush plants, welcoming candlelit tables, chairs, and accent lights that shine like fireflies. Ghost hunters who visit this place feel transported 100 years or more into the past. But they should be prepared to pay the price to dine in the four-star restaurant.

Orbs and other visual paranormal phenomena are often experienced by patrons of the world-famous Court of Two Sisters restaurant.

This is not the kind of place you can walk around, snapping pictures, and soaking up the atmosphere without being a patron.

The 600 block of Royal Street was once known as Governor's Row. As many as five Louisiana governors lived there at one time. Several judges, including a U.S. Supreme Court judge, resided on this block, too. The first resident of 613 Royal was Sieur Etienne de Perier, the royal governor of Louisiana from 1726 to 1733. In the 1880s, two sisters occupied this site. Living in quarters upstairs, they operated a *rabais,* a notions shop that dealt in dresses, gowns, lace, ribbons, and other female accoutrements. Against the tide of the time, Emma and Bertha Camors carried on their thriving business after marrying, while raising families, and adjusting to widowhood. They outlasted their husbands by several years. Emma and Bertha were born in 1858 and 1860, respectively, and died in 1944, within two months of each other. They are buried in St. Louis Cemetery Number 3.

The Camorses' shop catered to the social elite of New Orleans. They carried the latest fashions from Paris, with all the accessories to make the fancy ladies even more irresistible to the rich men of the city. Without doubt, much gossiping went on as schemes were hatched, rivalries revealed, and secret lovers named.

Ghost hunters have searched throughout the large restaurant for the Camors sisters, but there are no reports available that confirm their presence. Photographs, taken without disturbing diners in the luxuriant courtyard, have captured orbs and white, wispy clouds. In one photograph, two orbs were captured, hovering low near the ground. The spheres were slightly overlapped leading to speculation that these orbs are remnants of the two inseparable sisters.

GHOST OF THE RESTAURANT

Antoine's Restaurant
713 St. Louis Street
New Orleans 70130
504-581-4422
www.antoines.com

Antoine Alciatore arrived in New York in 1838 hoping the New

World would be the birthplace of his greatest dream. After two agonizing years in the big city, he realized that all things are possible, but only if you found the right place. Calling upon his French ancestry, he reckoned that the right place was the Paris of America, New Orleans. He arrived in the Crescent City in 1840 and took a job at the St. Charles Hotel. This afforded him a place to sleep, three meals a day, and opportunities to learn how business was done in this unique city. Later that same year, Alciatore opened his restaurant, offering cuisine that brought lasting success. Today, the restaurant he founded is a four-star success. It is the oldest family-owned and -operated restaurant in America. Several culinary triumphs are credited to its chefs, including oysters Rockefeller.

In 1868, Alciatore moved his restaurant down the block to its current location, acquiring neighboring buildings, knocking out a few walls, and finally expanding to its present configuration. This fantastic restaurant boasts a wine cellar of 25,000 bottles, four private dining rooms, and large banquet facilities. Success at the new location was wonderful but short lived. By 1874, Alciatore became gravely ill. Wishing to die in his native France and spare his family the spectacle of his deterioration, he bid his loved ones adieu and sailed for Marseilles. Soon after his arrival, he died. Alciatore's ghost, however, found passage back to New Orleans.

The ghost of Antoine Alciatore has remained on the premises for more than a century, watching over his beloved restaurant and the descendants who operate it. Dressed in a tuxedo, he has been seen in several dining rooms including the Japanese Room, the front dining room, and the Mystery Room.

The Mystery Room got its name during Prohibition. Regulars at the restaurant would enter the ladies' restroom and then pass through a secret door into a small room in which gin was dispensed in coffee cups. When asked where the drinks came from, patrons replied, "It's a mystery to me." Before long, the illegal bar became known as the Mystery Room. Antoine visits the Mystery Room regularly, although in his time, wine and spirits flowed like the waters of the nearby Mississippi.

Other ghosts have been detected in various parts of the restaurant. Apparitions have been spotted in the mirrors of both the men's and

The ghost of Antoine Alciatore still watches over the staff and patrons of the restaurant he opened in 1868.

women's restrooms. Finely dressed people in 19th-century clothing make brief appearances. Cold spots have been encountered in virtually every part of the restaurant. Ghost hunters will find this place fertile ground for investigations, but they should be prepared to pay for a meal.

ARNAUD'S RESTAURANT

813 Bienville Street
New Orleans 70112
504-532-5433
www.arnauds.com

A dashing, young Frenchman arrived in America late in the 19th century full of dreams and a resolve to do whatever it took to achieve them. His great ambition was to open a fine restaurant that reflected his personal philosophy of dining. According to the restaurant's Web site, young Arnaud Cazenave believed that "a meal that was only a meal was a shamefully wasted opportunity for enhancing one's life." To this aspiring restaurateur, food was a joy to the senses that would lead to "sound sleep, good health, and long life."

But newly arrived in bustling New York, Cazenave found himself working on the fringes of the restaurant industry. He made a living as a wine salesman, selling wine to the elegant restaurants of the Big Apple. This afforded Cazenave several opportunities to learn about the pitfalls and secrets of operating a restaurant, refine his plans, and decide on that essential element, location. For a Frenchman in America, that choice was easy.

Cazenave opened his New Orleans restaurant in 1918 and gave himself the title of count. As a testament to his philosophy of food and unique flare for dining, the restaurant achieved instant popularity. Expansions followed as Cazenave bought adjacent properties, some constructed in the late 1700s, and turned them into dining rooms and bars, all connected to the kitchen by circuitous passageways. As it turned out, this arrangement served restaurant patrons well, offering several exits and entrances and private dining rooms that made clandestine meetings with mistresses a thing of ease. Out of all of this, the count not only made a lot of money but accumulated a long list of patrons who owed him special favors for his discretion.

This restaurant was such an integral part of the count's life that he refused to let his death in 1948 tear him away from his great love. Patrons and restaurant staff have seen this dapper gentleman decked out in a stylish tuxedo. He appears in several locations, inspecting the tables, kitchen, bars, and service areas. It is said that this ghost offers expressions of great displeasure—from a raised eyebrow to scowls—if he finds spotted silver, creased napkins, or tables set without perfect symmetry. Numerous wait staff and busboys have had encounters with this meticulous restaurateur, especially if a tray is dropped or anything is spilled. The count always shows up when these rare events occur.

Another ghost at Arnaud's is believed to be that of his daughter, Germaine Cazenave Wells. Wells took over the restaurant when the count died, despite his concerns for her lifestyle, which centered on drinking and men. But Wells rose to the standard established by the count and contributed to the long life of the restaurant. Her ghost is spotted wearing a large hat and flowing gown. She hovers a few inches off the ground and is often seen leaving the ladies' room.

The many passageways that connect one dining area to another are good places to capture orbs or disks on film or hunt for cold spots, partial apparitions, and sensations of thickened atmosphere. These were the corridors to excitement, intrigue, or disaster for those who played risky games. Secret meetings started and ended here, leaving remnants ranging from odors of cigar smoke to the rustle of long gowns.

Several ghosts have been known to frequent the Richelieu Bar. The count has been spotted here, appearing in his trademark tuxedo, with other partial apparitions that are not easily described. Cold spots are also often experienced. At times, blasts of cold air fill the room, startling patrons. This part of the restaurant was once an opium den. Its spectral patrons may show up only to be surprised by the fine establishment created by Count Arnaud.

CHAPTER 4

The French Quarter—
East of Orleans Avenue

JANITOR ALWAYS ON DUTY

The Presbytere
751 Chartres Street
New Orleans 70116
504-568-6968

The Presbytere was built in 1797 by philanthropist Don Andres Almonester y Roxas and deeded to the Spanish colonial government as a commercial center. In 1834, during the early days of the American period, the Presbytere became a courthouse. Major renovations were made in 1847, including the addition of the mansard roof and interior changes to accommodate the needs of expanding legal activities. In 1911, the venerable old Presbytere became part of the Louisiana State Museum. Again, major renovations were made enticing old spirits to come and see what's new.

The janitor of the building probably liked his job. Rambling around the huge, old building at night when no one else was there may have given him a relaxing sense of space, a little freedom, and a rather large domain over which he alone presided. He probably liked the silence of the hallways and the old, heavy atmosphere of the large chambers. He was charged with the care and cleaning of a very old and important building, and he lived up to the responsibilities and continues to do so even after death.

Still wearing his uniform of dark pants and shirt, the ghost of the janitor walks the long halls and floats across the large rooms. Staff and visitors describe him as tall and slim, with curly light brown hair sometimes topped with a cap. He has been known to move house-keeping equipment not put away by current staff. This ghost has also been known to take a walk up St. Ann Street and visit people living in apartments nearby. It is said that he likes to watch young women in their apartments. Perhaps decades of lonely nights cleaning the Presbytere made him starved for female companionship.

Extensive reconstruction of the Presbytere, including replacing the old cupola on the roof, was completed August 28, 2005, one day before Hurricane Katrina. Of interest, this architectural element came down in a hurricane that struck the city September 29, 1915. Renovations often awaken spirits and result in news sightings of previously unknown spirits.

PERE DAGOBERT DE LONGUORY, THE SINGING MONK

Pirate's Alley between Chartres and Royal streets
New Orleans 70116

An hour or so after sunset, an amorphous mist rises from the ground at the end of Pirate's Alley at Chartres Street. As the mist begins to move toward St. Louis Cathedral, it takes the form of a shrouded figure, and footsteps are heard as invisible leather sandals pad along the damp pavement of the alley. Then, as the apparition becomes more solid, revealing the form of a short, stocky man dressed in the rough, brown robes of a Capuchin monk, the faint, melodic tones of a gifted baritone can be heard. Farther down the alley, the eerie voice grows louder and resonates off the walls of the cathedral and the Cabildo. The singing monk then turns, passes through the locked iron gate, and crosses St. Anthony's Garden on a path that parallels the back of St. Louis Cathedral. Sometimes, Pere Dagobert, the monk, stops, reverses his path, and begins another song.

Ghost hunters, working alone or with tours, have heard him sing entire performances of "Te Deum" or "Kyrie Eleison." To many, the singing monk appears lifelike and filled with the inspiration of the religious music he loves so much. His performances sometimes go on for hours before he climbs the steps at the rear of the cathedral and vanishes through a locked door.

The singing monk is one of the best-known and most-often-seen ghosts in the French Quarter. He is known not only for his magnificent voice, but also for his love for the people of old New Orleans. It was he, Pere Dagobert, who cared for the endless procession of sick who crawled up the steps of St. Louis Cathedral seeking medicine or final absolution. He fed the hungry, housed the homeless, and organized the community when disasters struck. And it was Pere Dagobert whose passion for religious music and gifted voice brought hundreds into the church on Sunday.

Pere Dagobert is best known for the great miracle he performed in October 1769. Three years earlier, the first Spanish governor, Don Antonio de Ulloa, arrived in New Orleans and was met with strong opposition by the city's wealthiest men and other prominent leaders, including Pere Dagobert, who refused to accept the fact that their beloved French city was no longer a French colony. Soon, an insurrection was staged, and Don Antonio escaped to Cuba. The citywide celebrations that followed were short lived, however. An angry King Carlos of Spain installed a stronger military governor, Don Alejandro O'Reilly, whom he backed with a fleet of 24 ships and 2,600 troops. In October 1769, as Spanish military rule fell over New Orleans, ten leaders of the insurrection were arrested, tried, and convicted of treason. On October 24, five of them were executed by a firing squad.

O'Reilly, in a move designed to crush the spirit of other rebels, ordered that the five corpses be left to rot on the levee, a few hundred feet from the steps of St. Louis Cathedral. For days, the bodies were exposed to the heat of the midday sun and dampness of evening rains. This despicable act appalled the citizens. Families of the dead begged O'Reilly for mercy—for a decent Catholic funeral and burial—but he refused. Then, the miracle occurred.

On a rainy night, Pere Dagobert went about town gathering the families of the dead. He ushered them into a room within the cathedral, gave them food and water, and told them to wait silently. Then, within view of Spanish soldiers guarding the levee and square in front of the cathedral, Pere Dagobert and a few followers removed the bodies from

Pere Dagobert performed a miracle near St. Louis Cathedral in October 1769. His ghost still lingers near the church.

the levee and carried them, in a solemn procession, across the square and down the alley to the back door of the church. As they walked, Pere Dagobert sang "Kyrie Eleison." He let his voice fill the square and alley, yet the Spanish soldiers heard nothing. Even Don Alejandro O'Reilly and his officers, comfortably ensconced in nearby houses, heard nothing.

When Pere Dagobert released the families from the dark room, they entered the church sanctuary, amazed to find their loved ones prepared for a Catholic funeral mass. Later, the procession carried the slain rebels to a cemetery were they were entombed. It was said that Pere Dagobert performed a miracle that night in October 1769, under the very noses of the Spanish soldiers who could have opened fire at any time on the singing monk and his followers.

Some tour guides and ghost hunters say that Pere Dagobert's evening concerts are simply a display of his musical talent performed because he loved to hear his voice echo off the walls of the cathedral. Others insist that this musical procession is a ghostly reenactment of his brave and solemn march from the bloodied execution site at the levee to the sanctuary of St. Louis Cathedral.

DUELING PISTOLS AND RESTLESS SPIRITS

St. Anthony's Garden
Royal Street behind St. Louis Cathedral
New Orleans 70116

This beautiful garden, filled with tall trees and tropical plants, covers the highest ground in the French Quarter. This probably accounts for the fact that it contains three in-ground graves, two of which are occupied. In the old days, when floods from levee breaks and heavy rains were frequent, this dry ground, sitting immediately behind St Louis Cathedral, was an attractive place to bury some of the earliest residents of New Orleans. As with other cemeteries in the region, tombstones were lost or never erected. Unmarked graves were often used during the deadly epidemics and fires of the late 18th century, when bodies accumulated in the streets. It is believed that hundreds of unmarked graves are contained within the iron fences of the old gardens. Some dispute this, citing proof that the alleged mass burial of a ship's crew never took place there. But to many, the peaceful, strange atmosphere of the gardens suggests something else is there besides beautiful plants.

Late at night, when street noise is minimal, visitors standing at the iron fence have seen shadows move across the ground and feel the puff of a cold breeze. Some sensitive visitors to St. Anthony's Garden also hear the pop and whine of bullets fired from old pistols. From about 1740 to 1790, this ground was the favorite location of the town's brazen young men for settling disputes and defending their honor. Duels fought here most likely resulted in horrible wounds and several deaths, but the environmental imprints detected by some ghost hunters were probably created by the excitement and fear that preceded the firing of shots. One of the best locations for experiencing this paranormal phenomenon is at the corner of Royal Street and Pere Antoine Alley.

The singing monk Pere Dagobert appears on this path through St. Anthony's Garden, filling the air with his baritone voice.

There is no official record of the duels fought here, but they were so frequent, and the pistols so noisy, that the priests of the cathedral stopped these affairs of honor. A new location was found in City Park (see Dueling Oaks in Chapter 5).

CIVIL WAR DEAD AND WOUNDED

Provincial Hotel
1024 Chartres Street
New Orleans 70116
504-581-1018

Strange, ghostly visions of Civil War soldiers are commonplace at the Provincial Hotel, particularly in rooms of building 500.

Several old structures comprise this stylish French Quarter hotel. Building 500 sits on land that belonged to the Ursuline Order of nuns who came to New Orleans in 1725. When the good sisters arrived, this plot of land, and the newly constructed military hospital there, came under their domain. Wounded American and British soldiers from the Battle of New Orleans were treated there, and an unknown number of soldiers died there. In the 1830s, lawyer Dominique Seghers purchased the land, tore down the Ursuline Hospital, and put up two large houses. In the late 1850s, the buildings were joined by a wide hallway and renovated to serve as a boarding house, coffee shop, and retail stores. During the Civil War, this large structure was commandeered by the military governor, Major General Benjamin Butler, for use as a military hospital. Scores of wounded were brought here from battles that took place in the Mississippi River valley as far away as Natchez and Florida.

Guests at the Provincial Hotel often encounter the ghosts of doctors and other medical staff walking about with blood-stained aprons. Soldiers walking with canes or crutches, arms in slings, and bandaged heads have been seen in the lobby, the courtyard, and several of the guest rooms of building 500. One guest reportedly stepped out of a shower and found piles of towels on the floor. Looking closer, she discovered they were bandages and sheets spotted with blood. It is common to find blood stains on carpets and walls that appear for only seconds and then vanish.

Another report tells of a security guard who stepped out of an elevator into an 1863 hospital ward full of wounded soldiers tended by several nurses. Moans and cries of the ailing men were answered by the nurses who raced from one patient to another. The astounded guard watched the bizarre scene for several minutes before walking backwards into the elevator.

THE OLD URSULINE CONVENT

1100 Chartres Street
New Orleans 70130
504-525-9585

From virtually every angle, the Old Ursuline Convent doesn't look its age. The graceful, classic architecture combined with excellent care by dedicated a staff and a little luck have helped this grand old building remain beautiful after more than 250 years. Completed in 1752, the convent survived fires that destroyed most of the French Quarter in 1788 and again in 1794. The convent also survived hurricanes and other natural disasters as well as the local French rebellion against Spanish rule in 1768. Throughout this long and often tumultuous history, the sisters of the Ursuline Convent have been angels of mercy to the disadvantaged of New Orleans. They cared for the sick during the cholera and yellow-fever epidemics, tended the wounded from the War of 1812, housed starving orphans who could no longer survive on the street, and nursed Civil War soldiers who took their last breath on Louisiana soil.

Today, the magnificent interior of the convent is predominantly a museum joined by St. Mary's Church, with its spectacular altar. In the foyer, a staircase salvaged from the original Ursuline Convent built in 1727 stands with well-worn treads. The stairs are closed to visitors, but ghosts of the Ursuline sisters are often seen passing between the first and second floors silently carrying out their duties. Ghost hunters have seen their apparitions, dressed in the traditional dark habits, with rosaries tied about their waists. Others have seen partial apparitions or sensed the presence of the sisters as they move about the nine rooms of the first floor, caring for the sick and dying. Psychic investigators have detected energy or the presence of many spirits in some of these rooms interpreted as the presence of sick and

The ghosts of Ursuline nuns have been seen descending the 200-year-old staircase of the Old Ursuline Convent.

injured children cut off from their families as a result of some disaster. A recent visit by a ghost hunter revealed the strong presence of many injured and frightened spirits in area eight, designated the Cultures of the Church room. Ghosts have been spotted in the upper floors, but these are generally off limits to most visitors. In the gardens, people have seen the partial apparition of a tall man in a blue uniform.

A HOST OF GHOSTS

Beauregard-Keyes House
1113 Chartres Street
New Orleans 70116
504-523-7257

From the street, this fascinating old house looks peaceful, as if little goes on here. The twin staircases to the wide front porch look as

Several ghosts haunt the historic Beauregard-Keyes House, including that of murdered mafioso, a general and his wife, and a cat named Caroline.

though no one has tread upon them for many years. But for decades, the Beauregard-Keyes House has been known for noisy hauntings. Named for two of its most famous occupants, Confederate general P. G. T. Beauregard and author Frances Parkinson Keyes, the house offers fascinating experiences for sensitive ghost hunters.

Built in 1826 by Joseph LeCarpentier, the house had had many owners until General Pierre Gustave Toutant Beauregard and his new wife, Caroline Deslonde, moved in May 1860. Later that year, after more than 15 years of service in the U.S. Army, the general was appointed commandant of the military academy at West Point. His orders called for him to take charge of the institution on February 1, 1861. With great sadness, Beauregard left Caroline in New Orleans, with the promise that their separation would only be temporary, and arrived at West Point on the eve of Louisiana's secession from the Union, January 26, 1861. With the country and its military hierarchy in the throes of bitter debates and sharp divisions that would soon culminate in civil war, the general's loyalties were called into question. After only five days in the commandant's chair, and with little consideration of his exemplary military service, Beauregard's appointment at West Point was revoked.

Caroline welcomed him home and planned a grand ball to be held in the spacious dining room of the Chartres Street home. But a commission in the Confederate army also awaited the general with an urgent summons to join President Jefferson Davis in the new Confederate capital, Montgomery, Alabama. Caroline's grand ball would have to wait, but Beauregard assured her he would return soon. As he rode away, he had no idea he would never see her alive again.

Within weeks, General Beauregard had deployed Confederate forces around Charleston Harbor, with every cannon trained on the Union fort in the middle of the bay. On April 12, 1861, Beauregard gave the order to fire on Fort Sumter, winning the opening battle of the Civil War. That victory was followed by another at Bull Run, but the general's horrible defeat at Shiloh in 1862 followed him until his death in 1893 and detracted from his place in the history of the Confederacy.

While fighting Union forces in Florida in 1864, the beleaguered general, weakened by a series of illnesses, received word that Caroline had died in New Orleans. Various newspapers aligned with the Union incessantly criticized Beauregard for leaving his sickly wife. These attacks plagued him for the rest of his life and left him depressed and somewhat detached from New Orleans society. Rumors were spread telling tales of the general wandering the house at night, calling out for Caroline, donning his uniform, and charging down the hallway, attacking any enemy he could find. Neighbors, acquaintances, and others, probably house servants, reported that the general also spent hours in the middle of the night pacing the huge dining room, as if Caroline's grand ball had, indeed, finally taken place.

Reports of these strange noises and ethereal images seen through shaded windows continued long after Beauregard's death. A tenant who later occupied the apartment under the main floor of the house reported the sounds of furniture being moved and music from an orchestra. No explanation could be found, as the main floor of the house was unoccupied. Others have heard ghostly remnants of

Caroline's grand ball, including music, the steps of dancers, and voices in celebration. The general's handsome silhouette, resplendent in his Confederate uniform, has been seen through the shaded windows of the dining room. He waltzes with the pale apparition of a lady believed to be Caroline.

Since the early 1950s, people associated with the house have reported the sounds of a battle coming from the wide hallway that passes from the front of the house to the rear. Some have interpreted these sounds as a ghostly reenactment of Beauregard's defeat at Shiloh. Cannon fire, pistol shots, the cries of wounded men, and clash of swords have given startled witnesses the impression that the house was full of Civil War ghosts. It is possible that these sounds were an environmental imprint or emotional remnants of Beauregard's midnight ramblings up and down the hall, during which he relived the bloody battle of Shiloh.

Other explanations have been offered for the ghostly sounds of pistol shots and shouts of wounded men. In June 1908, the Giacona family occupied the house, established themselves in a successful business, and became known for their dinner parties. While attracting the admiration of the neighbors, the Giaconas also attracted the attention of the local mafia, who tried to extort money from them. On the evening of June 17, 1908, the patriarch, Pietro, invited four members of the mafia to his home to discuss their demands. Soon after the mafioso were seated at a table in the rear gallery, Pietro and his son, Carrado, opened fire, killing three of them. The fourth man escaped, but was found later at a hospital, severely wounded. Local newspapers described the scene as a blood bath. The large amount of ammunition expended and numerous wounds found in the corpses are reminiscent of casualties of war. Some ghost hunters believe that the reports of pistol shots and shouts attributed to Beauregard's defeat at Shiloh may be ghostly remnants of the mafia massacre that took place in the rear gallery. I have detected a large cold spot on the gallery adjacent to the stairs that lead to the courtyard.

Frances Parkinson Keyes, the last famous resident of this house, may also be among the ghosts who reside here. Keyes moved there in 1940, when the house was virtually uninhabitable. Living in the old slave quarters, she restored the grand house, leaving an architectural

Ghosts of Civil War soldiers reenact their final battle in the central hallway of the Beauregard-Keyes House.

legacy in addition to a large collection of books, many of which she wrote while living here. Keyes died in 1971 in a small bedroom surrounded by her books, photographs of friends, and her little dog, Lucky. Days later, Lucky died, joining her mistress in the spirit world. But Lucky still roams the quarters behind the main house. Many visitors, including a guide dog for the blind, have detected his scent in a house long absent of canine residents.

A ghost cat named Caroline also appears in the gardens and main house, rubbing against the legs of tour guides. It is reported that this cat wears a bell around its neck but no one associated with the Beauregard-Keyes House admits to hearing it as the cat dashes through the courtyard.

THE OLD U.S. MINT

Louisiana State Museum
400 Esplanade Avenue
New Orleans 70116
504-568-6968

Renowned architect William Strickland designed this U.S. mint in the Greek Revival style reminiscent of upriver plantation mansions. Sitting at the very edge of the well-defined French Quarter, Strickland's design was not seen as a Yankee intrusion on the French-Caribbean style of the Vieux Carré. When it was completed in 1836, its spacious galleries, or porches, and strong, graceful lines created a visually pleasing transition to the Faubourg Marigny beyond grand Esplanade Avenue.

It is said that, during his presidency, Andrew Jackson ordered construction of this mint to establish a large federal agency at a place considered the edge of America's frontier. It is more likely that Jackson was repaying some political debts. U.S. currency and coin were struck here from 1838 to 1861. When Louisiana seceded from the Union in February 1861, state officials seized the property and minted Confederate money using Yankee machinery. Rebel troops were also housed there until New Orleans fell to the Union army in 1862. Part of the building was then used as military offices and barracks. After the war, federal minting resumed until 1909. Today, the building houses part of the collection of the Louisiana State Museum. It also houses a ghost or two.

As with any building that stood during the tumultuous times of war and other disasters, such as yellow-fever epidemics, some soldiers housed here and a few employees of the mint died on the premises. At least one of these fellows has remained long after his death. Standing on the corner of French Market Place and Barracks Street, visitors have a clear view of the second-floor gallery to the left. A tall, thin man dressed in blue coveralls or a blue uniform stands on the balcony rolling a cigarette. He places the cigarette in his mouth then walks the length of the gallery before vanishing through a wall. This pale blue apparition has been seen in broad daylight, but the apparition is most visible when shadows fall across the gallery.

THE CARRIAGE MASTER

Hotel St. Pierre
911 Burgundy Street
New Orleans 70116
504-524-4401
www.frenchquarterinns.com/hotelstpierre/

The carriage master of the Hotel St. Pierre was devoted to his duty. Resplendent in blue pantaloons, blue shirt, and polished boots, he was always at his post in the carriageway, handling the horses, harnesses, rigs, and wagons that passed in and out. Members of the Peyroux family, who owned the house, were constantly on the go and relied on the carriage master to have their conveyances ready at short notice.

Judging from his appearance, he died in his late 40s or early 50s. He was not a tall man, but he was quite muscular. We know this because the carriage master is still on duty more than 150 years after his death. The pale but complete apparition appears in the carriageway of the Hotel St. Pierre. He stands, watching the street, ready for the arrival of a rig pulled by tired horses. Ghost hunters may see this man any time of day but sightings are most likely when the carriageway is shaded from the sun. His presence at this location may be tied to the history of the structures that make up the hotel.

Gabriel Peyroux de la Roche purchased the property in 1780 with plans to erect a city dwelling. That same year, he constructed a house on his plantation on Bayou Road then had it partially dismantled and moved to the lot on Burgundy Street. The house now serves as the entry and office of the Hotel St. Pierre. Other Creole cottages were soon added, creating a large estate in the heart of the French Quarter. It is possible that the devoted carriage master worked on the Peyroux plantation, then moved to town when the master's house was relocated in 1780.

Scientific and psychic investigation of the carriageway ghost by the ISPR have turned up another entity on the property. These ghost hunters found the ghost of a Confederate soldier in a former slave quarters that stands across the street from the Hotel St. Pierre. Hotel guests who stay in these rooms have reported the sensation of an invisible entity sitting on the bed. One woman felt an icy cold hand touch her leg as she was about to fall asleep.

GHOST OF THE VOODOO PRIESTESS

1020 St. Ann Street
New Orleans 70116

Voodoo priestess Marie Laveau may be the most elusive ghost in New Orleans. This is at odds with her legacy, found in various shops, bookstores, souvenir stands, and bars throughout the French Quarter. There are occasional sightings of her ghost at St. Louis Cemetery Number 1, outside her cottage on St. Ann Street, walking the levee overlooking the Mississippi River, and at several other spots around town. It is said that she walks among the faithful to worship at church on St. John's eve (June 23), recognized by the colorful tignon, or headdress, that she wears. Her apparition may be barely discernible in the humid summer air or winter fogs of New Orleans, but many believe her voodoo magic is as powerful as ever, adding to the mystique of the Crescent City.

Marie Laveau, a free person of color, was born on Santo Domingo sometime between 1783 and 1794. The estimated date of her birth is at odds with the recorded date of her death, June 16, 1881. It seems improbable that she would have lived nearly 100 years, enduring numerous epidemics and other hardships.

Records at St. Louis Cathedral indicate that Laveau married Santiago "Jacques" Paris on August 4, 1819. A few years later, Paris died, leaving his young bride childless in a small cottage on Rampart Street. Within a year, the widow married the dashing Captain Christophe Duminy Glapion, with whom she had 15 children. In order to support this large family, Laveau worked as a hair stylist. She carried on this trade for many years, finding it incredibly lucrative.

Working within the homes of the French Quarter's wealthiest ladies afforded Laveau unparalleled opportunities to overhear gossip. She also served as a sounding board for frustrated women who aired their grievances, exposed their jealousies, named their rivals, and openly discussed schemes to win the hearts of lovers or engage in affairs. In little time, clever Laveau found a way to turn all of this information to her financial advantage. Some called it blackmail; others called it a skillful use of the weaknesses of others.

Marie Laveau also practiced the art of voodoo, a mystical West African religion based on the belief that all animate and inanimate objects possess a spiritual component, or ghost, which survives after death. Using the right incantations, rituals, lights, dances, props (such as snakes), beverages, and herbs, a voodoo practitioner can call on these ghosts or spirits to perform deeds on the earthly plane. These deeds might be harmless acts, such as causing a man to fall in love with a woman or turning a business deal to favor one party. But many believe darker purposes are also served, such as ruining a rival's business, influencing judicial decisions against the tide of justice, or causing fatal illnesses or accidents. Marie Laveau's considerable skills for obtaining private information added the illusion of magic to her voodoo cures, curses, plans, and rituals.

In contrast to her many private dealings, conducted for a substantial fee, the voodoo priestess also staged huge public ceremonies on the shore of Lake Pontchartrain. These ceremonies were complete with animal sacrifices, bizarre exhibitions, and dances. She also sold charms and gris-gris, magical substances blended together and contained within a small bag that can be concealed on one's person or secretly deposited into the pockets or purses of one's lovers or rivals.

Laveau was able to bridge the gap between her voodoo practices and the religious values of French Quarter citizens by incorporating many Catholic saints and symbols into her rituals and ceremonies. This skillful blending of cultural elements contributed to the acceptance of voodoo by many white citizens and made her a wealthy woman. For a sizeable fee, Laveau offered prayers to various saints and African spirits, asking them to work on behalf of a client. These spirits responded by revealing valuable information to her that was needed by the client, such as recipes for special potions, curses, or incantations. If the client was successful, Laveau claimed that her voodoo magic had invoked the intervention of powerful spirits. In return, her reputation, power, and business increased.

The voodoo legacy of Marie Laveau is best appreciated by taking

The voodoo priestess Marie Laveau lived in this St. Ann Street house while practicing rituals that are part of the mystique of New Orleans.

a tour of New Orleans locations that figure prominently in the life and practices of this mystical priestess. (See Appendix D.) Her ghost has been reported in stores along Rampart Street. She allegedly slapped a man who took too much time with his transaction in a shop there. Laveau lived in the neighborhood with her first husband. The Laveau cottage at 1020 St. Anne Street is believed to be haunted by the voodoo priestess and, perhaps, other ghosts. People claim to have witnessed ghosts performing mystical ceremonies at this location. Sightings such as this sound suspicious, but others have spotted the ethereal image of a woman matching Laveau's description, complete with tignon, walking the street in front of the cottage. The same image has appeared for many who have visited the Laveau-Glapion family tomb in St. Louis Cemetery Number 1. The tomb is easy to find. It is covered with voodoo *X*s and tributes that people have left for the high priestess.

LAFITTE'S BLACKSMITH SHOP

941 Bourbon Street
New Orleans 70116-9377
504-522-9377

New Orleans is a town full of myths and legends. Truth and fiction are given equal time and are often blended together, with superstition and fantasy thrown in, into an indecipherable amalgam, sometimes leaving serious historians baffled as to the real facts. A good example is the story of pirate Jean Lafitte. Part of the problem is that characters such as Lafitte often created or encouraged stories about themselves to impress enemies, interest business associates, charm the ladies, or confuse government officials.

All of this came easy to the dashing French pirate because he wore many hats. He is best known as a hero of the Battle of New Orleans. But he was also a business associate of certain well-respected plantations owners, a property owner, slave smuggler, thief, pirate, kidnapper, drug dealer, and cheat. He is rumored to have been a murderer, too, but there is no proof that he ever took a human life. There is little doubt, however, that his band of pirates killed many innocent people.

From the standpoint of history, confusion surrounds virtually every pivotal point of Lafitte's life. He was born between 1780 and 1785 in the coastal city of Marseilles or a tiny village in northern France. Some reports say he was born in Port-au-Prince, Haiti. Confusion persists about his death, too. He is said to have died in the 1820s in Texas, the Yucatan Peninsula of Mexico, somewhere at sea, or in Illinois in 1844, where he lived under an assumed name. His final resting place is also unknown, but it is rumored to be at Berthoud Cemetery in the pirate village of Barataria in south Louisiana, at the bottom of the Caribbean, or somewhere on the Yucatan Peninsula.

Historical records have verified some aspects of Lafitte's life. Jean and his brother, Pierre, arrived in New Orleans about 1809 and set up a blacksmith shop in the French Quarter. The business was only a front for their smuggling operation. Within a few years, Jean and Pierre, with Captain Dominique You, headed a large gang of pirates based in Barataria Bay, south of the city. From this base, they raided ships throughout the Gulf of Mexico, taking anything of value, including slaves. The pirates melted down much of the gold and silver at the blacksmith shop, while art treasures and slaves were sold at secret meetings with rich plantation owners as far north as Opelousas. The Lafitte brothers also made money by selling stolen ships' goods to merchants in New Orleans, such as lamp oil, exotic wood, furniture, and metal objects.

Jean Lafitte's invaluable service in the Battle of New Orleans is also an established fact. He supplied men and supplies to the rag-tag American army as it faced more than 5,000 British troops supported by naval units on the Mississippi. As an expression of his gratitude, General Andrew Jackson obtained a presidential pardon for Lafitte and his band of pirates. Soon after the war, though, the restless pirate left New Orleans and set up a base at Galveston, Texas.

As with any pirate, rumors of hidden treasure have long survived the perpetrator and led to wild speculation about its location and value. Years ago, treasure hunters nearly destroyed Destrehan Plantation seeking Lafitte's gold. From time to time, people have speculated that valuables are hidden under the floor of Lafitte's Blacksmith Shop.

As for Lafitte's ghost, sightings have been reported at several locations. Those who claim to have seen him at the Blacksmith Shop on Bourbon Street have been ridiculed with the suggestion they were under the influence of bottled spirits instead of the presence of a ghostly spirit. Still, some have detected a disembodied presence in the room to the left at the rear of the little building. Not long ago, a sensitive ghost hunter detected a tall man with long, black hair and a full beard. The ghost seemed confused by the street traffic and modern bar with its electric lights and other amenities. The tall ghost doesn't move around much. He simply appears briefly, in the shadows of the back room, looks about the place with an expression of confusion on his face, and then vanishes.

Ghost hunters will have the best opportunity for experiencing the strange atmosphere and palpable history of Lafitte's Blacksmith Shop, and the ghostly presence of a tall man by visiting the place soon after

Pirate Jean Lafitte operated a blacksmith's shop in this building on Bourbon Street as a front for his illicit trade in stolen goods.

it opens in the morning. Most French Quarter bars are crowded and full of revelry by midafternoon.

LITTLE GIRL LOST IN THE MIRROR

Lafitte Guest House
1003 Bourbon Street
New Orleans 70116
504-581-2678

In the 19th century, many people in Louisiana, and elsewhere, believed that immediately after death, the soul of the deceased could enter a nearby mirror and become trapped there for eternity. To prevent this, all the mirrors in houses were covered with black cloths as the sick took their final breaths or were covered immediately after a sudden, unexpected death. At the Lafitte Guest House, and other places such as the Myrtles in St. Francisville, ghostly activity has resulted from a mirror that was not covered at the critical moment.

For years, the image of a little girl appeared in a large mirror on the second-floor hallway of the Lafitte Guest House. As guests and staff members walked toward the mirror, the little girl appeared to be standing behind them crying. When the surprised people turned around, expecting to find a lost child, she was gone. The little girl has also been sighted floating out of room 22 into the hallway next to the mirror. The pale apparition of the child has been caught on film at least four times, and her movements reenacted for the documentary *Haunted Louisiana*.

The large mirror that hung for more than a century at Lafitte Guest House has since been removed from the hallway. When I questioned a staff member, he could provide no explanation for this action. He mentioned, however, that sightings of the little girl have diminished since the mirror was removed, but they do still occur.

It is believed that the sad apparition in a pale, white gown is the ghost of five-year-old Marie, daughter of Paul Joseph Gleises and his wife, Marie Odalie Ducayet. Marie was one of thousands of New Orleans children who died during the yellow-fever epidemics of 1853 and 1854.

The ghost of a little girl named Marie haunts this second-floor landing in the Lafitte Guest House.

Research by ghost hunter and guide Tom Duran turned up four other girls named Marie who lived in this house at various times during the 1800s. It is known that the Gleises had six children and that three of them died in early childhood. It is possible that the girls all had the same first name, being distinguished by the middle name. This was a common practice in old Louisiana. Of course, it is possible that during the Civil War, when the Gleises resided in New York, another family occupied the house with one or more girls named Marie.

Marie prefers to stay close to the doorway of room 22. Research indicates this room and room 21 at the front of the house were the children's rooms. She has been seen on the stairs, treading the final steps to the second-floor landing. She appears to be crying and gives sensitive witnesses the impression that she is lost. Now that the mirror has been removed from its spot at the head of the hallway, little Marie may be more confused than ever.

MAD MADAM LALAURIE

Lalaurie Mansion
1140 Royal Street (at Governor Nicholls Street)
New Orleans 70116

The Lalaurie Mansion is believed to be the most haunted house in New Orleans. That's quite a reputation in a town known for ghostly activity, paranormal phenomena, and old, spooky buildings. The persistence of the reputation—for more than 150 years—is even more amazing since the place has been a private residence for decades, and visitors who inquire about ghosts are not especially welcome. But then, some of the ghostly activity associated with this mansion can be viewed from the street. In fact, several people viewing the building with French Quarter ghost tours have simultaneously observed two ghosts who are central characters in the gruesome history of this bizarre place.

Standing on Governor Nicholls Street on the opposite sidewalk, ghost hunters have seen the spectral reenactment of Madam Delphine Lalaurie, with a whip in her hand, chasing a slave girl across the rear galleries of the house late in the evening in 1832. The event, reported in detail by contemporary writers in city newspapers and retold in 1882 by journalist George W. Cable, started when the slave girl pulled the madam's hair while brushing her long, red locks. Incensed, Madam Lalaurie chased the frail little girl from her bed chamber, onto the rear gallery, whipping her for the slight irritation. Screaming and clinging to the balcony, the seven year old suffered blow after blow until she could no longer stand the pain. To some witnesses, standing on the opposite sidewalk, it appeared that the little girl jumped to her death while others reported that the force of the blows caused her to slip through the rails of the balcony and fall more than 30 feet to the courtyard.

A few of Madam Lalaurie's neighbors, whose attention was attracted by the screaming slave, gathered as she inflicted the horrible punishment. Some called out, demanding that she stop, and threatened to summon the police. But wealth and high social position together

Madam Delphine Lalaurie and her husband, Louis, committed atrocities on their slaves in the attic of this mansion.

with a high wall surrounding the courtyard protected Madam Lalaurie from her protesting neighbors and immediate police inquiry. She had enough time to bury the slave in a shallow pit in the courtyard before the officers arrived a day or two after the heinous event.

When confronted with statements made by witnesses, Madam Lalaurie denied the event ever took place. The brief police investigation failed to turn up a body or any sign that a slave had been mistreated. Before long, Delphine and her physician husband, Louis, resumed their parties and grand dinners, quickly dissipating rumors that she mistreated her slaves. But on April 11, 1834, a fire broke out in the kitchen that exposed the horrors hidden within the Lalaurie Mansion.

That evening, a 70-year-old cook, confined to the kitchen by a 25-foot chain, reached the limit of her endurance. Starvation in the midst of elegant and plentiful food, the whippings, wounds, murders, and stories whispered among the house slaves about a secret torture room on the third floor finally made death more attractive than life. The old woman set fire to the kitchen table then spread the flames to the lard bucket and coal pile. In minutes, the Lalaurie Mansion was filled with smoke.

Police, neighbors, and firefighters rushed to the scene. As the flames were subdued, Madam Lalaurie directed an army of volunteers to save the valuable art, furniture, china, crystal, and other treasures. She dismissed inquiries about her slaves and replied, "Never mind them now. Save the valuables."

Incensed by Madam Lalaurie's callous disregard for the well-being of her slaves, prominent New Orleans citizens Judge Canonge, M. Montreuil, M. Lefebre, and Señor Fernandez worked their way through the thick smoke to the second and third floors searching for anyone they might save from suffocation. On the third floor, they discovered a heavy, locked door that led to an attic. Acting on their suspicions, they broke through the door and discovered a scene that is among the most gruesome in the history of slavery. The room contained ten slaves, all in a state of advanced starvation. Some were caged liked animals, with hideous bone malformations, the result of Dr. Lalaurie's medical experiments. Others were chained to the walls. Some of these poor souls had gaping wounds infested with maggots.

Two slaves, a man and woman, were found with their genitals surgically removed and sewn onto the slave of the opposite sex. Other atrocities included plucked-out eyeballs, mouths stuffed with animal dung, lips sewn shut, abdomens opened, intestines wrapped around the chest, and an open head wound through which a man's brain could be stirred with a stick. Aside from all that, the horrible stench nearly drove the four rescuers from the room.

Eventually, seven slaves were removed alive from the Lalaurie torture chamber. At least three died during efforts to carry them from the house. Those who were alive were taken to the Cabildo and given medical care. The next day, as many as 4,000 citizens reportedly visited the slaves to see for themselves proof of the Lalaurie atrocities. Their anger became greater when the skeletons of 25 slaves, including children, were found under the flagstones of the courtyard. Indignation was so great that a mob formed and descended on the mansion that stood with little damage from the smoky fire. They smashed furniture, ripped wallpaper and art from the walls, broke windows, and destroyed elegant stair rails and balustrades.

During all of this, Delphine and Louis Lalaurie escaped detainment by the police and arraignment by the courts. Under the noses of a mob that loitered for days outside the mansion, they slipped out the side gate of their infamous courtyard and escaped from New Orleans to Lake Pontchartrain. Legend has it that they boarded a schooner that happened to be ready to sail and arrived a few days later in Mobile, Alabama. There, they established a power of attorney that empowered a New Orleans lawyer to close their business affairs. Then, they boarded a ship headed for France.

The departure of the Lalauries from New Orleans did not end the horrible social wounds caused by the despicable medical experiments they conducted on their slaves. In fact, this event fueled the antislavery movement while standing as bold evidence that money and social status could place the elite of New Orleans citizenry above the law.

Before the ashes cooled in the mansion, stories began to circulate around the French Quarter of strange, ghostly events. People in the neighborhood reported hearing cries and screams coming from the vacant house. The ghostly apparitions of slaves were seen on the balconies or standing in the windows. Years later, after the structure was

The ghost of a slave girl has been spotted on the rear galleries of the Lalaurie Mansion moments before she falls to her death.

rebuilt, the first tenants lasted only a short time. They left after encountering ghostly slaves in chains who walked the hallways. They reported that children who entered the house were chased by a spectral hand that wielded a whip.

The stories, rumors, and verified witness accounts continue to accumulate more than 150 years after the Lalaurie torture room was opened. Ghost hunters and passersby catch glimpses of Madam Lalaurie chasing the slave girl across the rear gallery. Slaves crying out in agony are often heard. Some sensitive ghost hunters have detected the environmental imprints of the April 10, 1834, fire and the riot that occurred the next day. Some people have heard the sound of wooden objects hitting the pavement together with the sound of windows being broken. The best vantage point to experience paranormal activity at the Lalaurie Mansion is on Governor Nicholls Street on the sidewalk opposite the mansion. Here, patient, sensitive ghost hunters sometimes experience a remnant of the frightful event that unlocked the Lalaurie secrets. Block out the sounds of the city and listen for the whimpering of the slave girl and the crack of Madam Lalaurie's whip.

LAYERS OF GHOSTS

Andrew Jackson Hotel
919 Royal Street
New Orleans 70116
504-561-5881

Several ghosts from different time periods have been detected at the charming Andrew Jackson Hotel. For ghost hunters, this location serves as a good example of multiple spirit remnants. These spirits often occupy newer structures that replaced the buildings linked to their deaths or some important event of their lives. They wander about the newer structures—a house, store, inn, factory, or fort—and appear oblivious to their new surroundings. They appear to walk through walls, following invisible paths that they walked when they were alive, or they appear knee deep in a pond recently constructed, for example.

In 1794, a boarding school for boys stood on the land now occupied by the Andrew Jackson Hotel. As a result of hurricane damage to part of the building, a fire broke out. The flames swept through the structure, killing five boys. Their ghosts still play in the courtyard and sometimes roam the hallways of the hotel. Guests have reported the loud laughter of children at play, the heavy footfalls of children running, and their voices calling out to each other. Sensitive ghost hunters have spotted apparitions of the boys passing through walls as they leave the courtyard. There are also reports of terrible screams. These are likely environmental imprints of the disastrous fire.

After the rubble was cleared, a courthouse was constructed at this location. The most famous person to appear in this court was Major General Andrew Jackson. After the War of 1812, in which he saved New Orleans from British invasion, Jackson was indicted for obstruction of justice and, later, contempt of court. The sad ghost who haunts the current building, however, is nameless. He is seen as a partial apparition in a corner of the courtyard, standing with his head bowed. His hands appear to be tied behind his back. When he appears, ghost hunters report a sad, oppressive atmosphere. It is likely he was found guilty of a capital crime and hanged at this location.

Sometime in the 1840s, the courthouse was torn down or destroyed by flood, fire, or storm. In its place, the current structure was built and opened as a hotel and boarding house. The unseen presence of a female can be detected in some of the rooms. She may have been a housekeeper or owner of the establishment because she seems quite interested in details of how the hotel is run. Items such as chairs, pillows, and towels are straightened if left slightly out of place. Busy housekeeping staff members often get the feeling that someone is watching them or standing directly behind them.

Ghosts from several tragedies haunt the popular Andrew Jackson Hotel, named for the hero of the Battle of New Orleans.

GHOST OF THE OCTOROON MISTRESS

734 Royal Street
New Orleans 70130

Just about every ghost-tour guide in the French Quarter tells the story of a wealthy young man and his beautiful mistress, a girl of mixed race. It shows up in books about haunted New Orleans and seems to be the stuff of legend. Ghost hunters are interested in the story of these two lovers because, it is said, their relationship took a tragic turn and the young lady ended up as a ghost, shivering on a rooftop through cold December nights or roaming through a tea room. The real value of the story is the example it serves of social mores of 1850 New Orleans, a town known then, as now, for its free-wheeling lifestyles that are sometimes at odds with strong Southern traditions.

The octoroon mistress was named Julie. Her ancestry included an African-American, making her one-eighth black and seven-eighths white. Women of this racial make-up were among those labeled free people of color and not afforded the rights and privileges of a white person. In fact, open relationships between white men and octoroons, as they were labeled, were not acceptable to rich families from the river plantations or the town's Creole elites who considered their bloodlines part of their wealth. Yet, it was widely known that young men fancied octoroons. The women were known for their beauty, and many of them were educated and well-schooled in the social graces. Masked balls and other semiprivate social events were regularly staged to provide opportunities for young gentlemen to enjoy the charms of these special ladies and, perhaps, select a mistress.

The attention of a wealthy man brought octoroon women financial support that might last many years, a comfortable furnished apartment or cottage, a slave or two, fine food and wine, and many other luxuries that were, by strong social tradition, reserved for whites only. The young men often maintained traditional families at home and kept their liaisons secret. Men of the city might see their mistresses several times each week while plantation gentlemen might enjoy their charms only when they were in town.

Julie was set up in a fine apartment on the third floor of 734 Royal Street. The young man's name is lost to history, but it is believed he was an unmarried Creole who resided in the city, living off the wealth of his family's plantation. Still, he was very much under the influence of his family and its traditions. He stood a good chance of losing their financial support and his promised inheritance if he should be so bold as to bring a girl of mixed race into the family by marriage. Julie was well aware of the limits of her relationship with the young man. But over a period of years, her love for him grew to such intensity that she could think of nothing other than becoming the wife of a Creole gentleman.

Julie brought up the issue many times, insisting she could not live unless she became his wife. Each time, the man insisted that marriage was impossible. He reminded her that he was dependent on his family for his livelihood and his parents would never allow such a union. New Orleans society was highly segregated at the time, still dependent on slavery, and easily outraged by the idea of a marriage of two people of different races. Secret liaisons were commonplace, but they must be kept secret and out of the public's eye or an entire family would suffer for a young man's romantic actions.

But still she asked, begged, and cried in his arms each time he refused her. Finally, he proposed a challenge as a way of putting an end to the issue, never thinking she would accept it. If Julie would spend a December night on the rooftop, naked, he would take her hand in marriage. Assuming the stunned look on her face meant she would never do such a foolish thing, he fell asleep. In the morning, though, he found her missing from the bed. He searched the apartment. On the floor, near the door to the attic, he found her nightgown. As he climbed the narrow stairs, a dark foreboding crept over him. As he stepped onto the roof, he found her lifeless body, naked and frozen.

Somehow the story got out. It might have been forgotten as the Civil War brought greater concerns to south Louisiana at that time. But people began to talk about the young naked woman seen on the rooftop at 734 Royal Street on the coldest of December nights. Julie's ghost, or an environmental imprint of her experience, has been seen there, shivering in the final minutes of her life, struggling to meet the young man's challenge and fulfill her greatest dream. To this day, people report seeing her as she walks along the edge of the roof. The ghost is visible from the street, but the best vantage points are those that afford a larger view of the roof. It is said that Julie appears about midnight, only on the coldest of December nights.

For those not able or willing to stand watch in cold, damp air, Julie might be found on the ground floor. She was detected there by psychic Otis Biggs, who maintained a small fortune-telling business in the Bottom of the Cup Tea Room. Biggs reported that he heard Julie tapping her fingernails on his table and encountered her particular perfume. Biggs and others have seen her reflection in the pond located in the courtyard and part of her yellow skirt as she passes through doorways.

In May 2005, this building at 734 Royal Street was empty and for sale. New tenants may accommodate ghost hunters who wish to investigate the courtyard pond and the rooftop. For now, living souls who search for the ghost of Julie must do so from the street or balconies of adjacent buildings.

As a side note, ghost hunters will find the Bottom of the Cup Tea Room on the opposite side of the block at 327 Chartres Street (504-524-1997). It offers rare teas and features a psychic who will tell your fortune. Some believe Julie has moved to this location, too. Her portrait hangs on the wall, reminding visitors of her beauty and of days when the strict social rules of old New Orleans brought an end to this secret love affair.

THE STREET THAT WAS ONCE A MORGUE

626 St. Phillip Street
New Orleans 70116

At night, the 600 block of St. Phillip Street looks peaceful enough. Calm, you might say, in spite of the foot traffic. As the evening wears on the atmosphere becomes strangely still. Even the revelry flowing out of Flanagan's Pub, across the street, doesn't drive away the stillness and the quiet sadness that sensitive ghost hunters experience.

The building at 626 is vacant now. It was a bar until recently. One hundred fifty years ago it was a morgue, and in the summer of 1853, the St. Phillip Street morgue was full of victims of the yellow-fever epidemic. In fact, the number of dead was so great—eventually reaching 11,000—that every morgue in the city was full. Bodies began to pile up on the streets. St. Phillip Street was so filled with bodies that they lay in stacks, four or five high, until caskets became available. The bodies filled the street, leaving little more than a deer trail down the middle for cemetery crews to pass.

Grieving families, having no recourse, left their loved ones wrapped in blankets or sheets labeled with toe tags. They did their duty, then lingered for a moment for one last touch. It would be a fleeting touch, with a longing to rescue the dearly departed from the clutches of death but fearful that touching might spread the lethal illness. These emotions were, somehow, imprinted on the environment.

Construction crews built many crematories and more cemeteries, and grave diggers finally caught up with the demand, but the miserable experience evoked strong emotions from anyone venturing past St. Phillip Street. The environmental imprint is so strong that it remains there today for sensitive ghost hunters and psychics to discover. Visitors have felt intense cold spots, thickened atmospheres that evoke intense sadness, and a sense of loss. They have detected fear, too. No one could have viewed the stacks of bodies without wondering if he would soon be among them.

CHAPTER 5

City Park, Faubourg Marigny, Treme, and Chalmette

Faubourg Marigny (pronounced *MA-ra-nee*) is the quiet neighborhood downriver from the boisterous French Quarter. Separated from the Vieux Carré by Esplanade Avenue, the neighborhood is framed by St. Claude Avenue, Press Street, and the mighty Mississippi. It was developed by a Creole millionaire Count Bernard Xavier Philippe de Marigny de Mandeville between 1803 and 1810. Anticipating a population explosion after the Louisiana Purchase of 1803, the count subdivided his family's plantation, laid out a grid of streets, and financed the construction of several mansions and business establishments, including one of the region's first casinos. The district became known as the Third Municipality of New Orleans. Creole gentlemen often housed their mistresses here and immigrants from northern states and the Caribbean set up residences and businesses.

The area became a more desirable neighborhood in 1831, when the Pontchartrain Railway was built down the center of Elysian Fields Avenue. Named after the Champs-Élysées in Paris, this avenue was the first street in New Orleans to reach Lake Pontchartrain five miles away. Esplanade Avenue is the major thoroughfare that conducts traffic from the district to City Park.

In the first half of the 20th century, the neighborhood was in decline, but most of the older houses survived. Since the 1984 World's Fair, Faubourg Marigny has undergone a slow redevelopment that has attracted new residents and businesses. Several live music venues, inns, and restaurants make the district a population destination for visitors now.

After passing through Faubourg Marigny and heading downriver to St. Bernard Parish, Chalmette Battlefield sits to the right of the highway. Here, in 1815, General Andrew Jackson whipped the British and saved New Orleans. Further downriver is the lower Mississippi bayou country known for its slower pace of life, rich natural habitats, and Woodland Plantation, the only remaining downriver manor house.

THE GHOST OF MADAME MINEURECANAL

2606 Royal Street
New Orleans 70116-2003

Little is known about Madame Mineurecanal. For years, the quiet lady was a familiar figure in the Marigny neighborhood, often seen walking her little white terrier, politely nodding to people she passed, but never stopping for conversation. No one knew of her miseries, her losses, or her failures. It was rumored that her husband was killed in the Spanish-American War of 1898 and her son left home and was never heard from again. Years after she was gone, people misplaced Madame Mineurecanal in history, claiming she was the wife of Count Bernard Marigny, who developed the neighborhood in the early 1800s. It is known that Madame Mineurecanal died in the first decade of the 20th century, a few years after losing the last of her family. The way she died has tied her to her house and the miseries she suffered.

Late one afternoon, after walking and feeding her loving terrier, Madame Mineurecanal climbed the steep stairs to the third-floor attic, moving slowly, weighted down with the burden of her decision. She stood on a chair as she fastened a rope on a ceiling beam to create a noose. As she placed the noose around her neck, her little dog began to whimper, sensing something bad was about to happen. Looking down at her faithful companion, she knew she could not leave the little dog alone in the house. She pulled the rope from her neck, stepped off the chair, and lifted the little dog, holding him to her chest. After a few gentle words, she strangled him, believing she would find the little dog waiting for her in the world beyond.

Climbing once more onto the chair, Madame Mineurecanal

placed the noose around her neck and kicked the chair away. With limbs flailing about and eyes bulging, her life was extinguished in a few horrible minutes. Whatever she wished to escape, the act of suicide has held her to the place where she lived alone, with only her little dog for company.

Stories about the haunted house and the mysterious Madame Mineurecanal started to circulate after World War II. The house was crowded with the large extended Ruez family whose presence may have been too stressful for the spirit of the "suicide madame." Nearly everyone in the Ruez family saw apparitions or heard strange sounds at night. Madame Mineurecanal—called "Mini Canal" by children living in the house—appeared in a white dress, with long dark hair and a ghastly expression on her face with her eyes bulging and tongue hanging from her gasping mouth. Her neck appeared bent, as if the bones were dislocated by the noose. Mini Canal appeared on the second-floor hallway, descending the attic stairs, in the bedrooms, and even at the front door. She was often seen with her pet terrier. Strange sounds reported there included the patter of dogs' feet, a woman's moaning and crying, creaking sounds coming from the attic that mimic a rope stretched over a wooden beam, and disembodied footsteps.

Sightings by Ruez family members were seldom pleasant. Most sightings were frightening and associated with bad luck, including a stillborn birth, death in a car accident, serious emotional problems, and a failed suicide attempt. A small child was found hanging by one hand from a balcony while another nearly strangled after falling from his highchair. Grandmother Ruez had the house blessed, but the ghostly activity continued.

In the mid-1990s, the house was purchased by Phil Hantel, a young attorney from another haunted town, Santa Fe, New Mexico. In a 1998 interview with reporter Jim Kane, Hantel reported that the previous owner—an American Indian—died of unknown causes in the house. The man's relatives performed rituals to release his soul and any other souls caught in the house. Then, the relatives burned juniper branches and sage and sang incantations throughout the house, driving any remnant spirits into the chimney, which they sealed. Hantel said that neighbors who witnessed the ceremonies advised him never to open the chimney.

Mini Canal may have been banished from the house, but her spirit still walks the narrow street as she takes her pet dog for a late afternoon stroll. Some people have detected strange cold spots and disembodied footsteps on the sidewalk near the house at 2606 Royal Street.

GHOSTLY BACON AND EGGS

Marigny Guest House
615 Kerlerec Street
New Orleans 70116-2003
888-696-9575
www.lamothehouse.com

It's like coming home to a cozy house, with Grandma in the kitchen, Papa Stanley tinkering in his room, and quiet 17-year-old Martha lost in her own world behind the closed door of her bedroom. To make it even more inviting, the enticing aroma of bacon and eggs drifts out of the kitchen. It feels so homey, so comfortable, so full of life, except the people you find here are all dead. It doesn't seem to matter that their home has become a restful bed-and-breakfast inn. These spirits are too attached to the place to move on.

According to legend, Papa Stanley, Grandma, and Martha went for a drive one evening to enjoy the cool air and get away from the crowded neighborhood. But their excursion ended in disaster, when they died in a collision with another car. Being a small, close-knit family, with strong ties to their Marigny house, the trio came home and continued as if nothing happened.

The innkeeper and some of the guests believe that this ghost family remains in the house, making their presence known in charming and sometimes comical ways. Grandma has been known to plant a gentle kiss on the cheeks of guests or the inn's owner as they settle down for a night's sleep. She has been seen standing at the top of the stairs. Psychics who have visited the house report that the woman generates a sense of sadness.

Papa Stanley seems to be friendly and quick to express his dissatisfaction with rude or obnoxious people. Reports state that one fellow was struck in the head with an empty soda can after making an offensive remark. For those people he likes, this ghost shows his affection by patting them on the shoulder or rear end. Psychics say that Stanley often uses words that might cause more modest people to blush, especially when he complains about the transformation of his special room into guest quarters. He thinks the curtains and bedding are too fancy and feminine.

Martha tends to stay in her room, sitting on the bed. Her face is often seen from the outside as she gazes out the window at the street. This ghost has been located by electromagnetic field detectors and psychics who get the impression that she is a loner, quiet and withdrawn.

THE GENTLE DOORMAN

Lamothe Guest House
621 Esplanade Avenue
New Orleans 70116
888-696-9575
www.lamothehouse.com

Most of the elegant townhouses and mansions that line Esplanade Avenue were built by the second wave of northerners who relocated to the Crescent City. The first wave, coming soon after the Louisiana Purchase in 1803, built their mansions on land that later became known as the Garden District. Members of the second wave brought money and business skills and sustained their wealth by opening banks, brokerages, investment houses, and shipping industries. They constructed houses similar to those found in the Garden District. They also built townhouses with side galleries, similar to those built in Charleston, South Carolina. Scattered among the newcomers in the neighborhood were a few locals, such as the famous Josie Arlington. Josie built or purchased homes along Esplanade in an effort to gain entry to high social circles or simply enjoy the comforts bought with money gained by sin, vice, or corruption.

The Lamothe House, built in the 1830s, stands on Esplanade in quiet elegance, across the street from the busy Vieux Carré. The beautiful

The ghost of a polite doorman haunts the foyer of the Lamothe House.

but modest façade gives the impression that the house is not large, but once inside, the array of hallways connects a large number of rooms that total more than 6,000 square feet. At the entry, a formal foyer, complete with black and white checkered floor tiles, welcomes guests to the townhouse that is now a popular bed-and-breakfast inn. Aside from the beautiful decor of the foyer, something else awaits guests that may be seen by sensitive ghost hunters.

The ghost of an old, black gentleman has been detected in the foyer. People have seen him rising from his chair and walking to the door as if to greet visitors. As he approaches the door, he vanishes. When questioned, staff members deny any knowledge of a doorman, ghostly apparitions, or other paranormal phenomena in the foyer. Psychic investigation, however, has revealed the presence of a man named Jeffrey or Geoffrey. He moves from his chair to the door, sometimes creating a patch of cool air.

Other rooms in the Lamothe House may also be fertile ground for ghost hunting. The great dining room on the second floor has an intriguing atmosphere, as does the curving staircase. Ghost hunters who are interested in the Faubourg Marigny may find this inn a perfect place for accommodations, as well as a starting point for their investigations.

THE FASTIDIOUS GENTLEMAN

Lanaux Mansion
547 Esplanade Avenue
New Orleans 70116-2016
504-488-4640
e-mail: lanaux@historiclodging.com

The fastidious gentleman Charles Andrew Johnson loved his Renaissance Revival townhouse located steps beyond the edge of the French Quarter. Without a wife or children for whom to care, he devoted much of his time to decorating the place with furnishings gathered during trips to Europe. When at home, he poured through magazines and books, making notes in the margins about color schemes, furniture arrangements, window treatments, and countless details that would make his home stylish and elegant. The practice of law was Johnson's profession, but decorating was his passion. Having spent years and a small fortune fitting the 12,000-square-foot mansion to his exact specifications and tastes, it is no surprise that Johnson declined to move out after his death in 1896.

The current owner, Ruth Bodenheimer, has seen Johnson's ethereal image ascending the stairs to the third floor. She feels his presence throughout the house and believes he provided valuable guidance during the years she restored the house to its 1879 glory. On numerous occasions, when Bodenheimer was debating issues such as paint color or style or type of furniture, she either pondered the questions or spoke them aloud. With little delay, Bodenheimer would be drawn to Johnson's collection of papers, magazines, or books, where she would find the answer. Johnson's reply was usually a margin note he had penciled or an underscored passage that provided whatever information was needed to continue the restoration of the house. Bodenheimer says these little chats were vital to her success in finding just the right rug, drapes, or paint color.

In 1991, Johnson's portrait was returned to the home and hung in a prominent location. In looking at it, you get the feeling that the fastidious gentleman is surveying the elegant rooms around him. His likeness conveys a sense of pride and kindly eyes. One wonders why such a gentleman, successful in the practice of law and a popular member of high society, never married. It may be that the woman he loved was already taken.

Various historical sources suggest that Johnson was enamored with his partner's daughter, Marie Andry Lanaux. Being a gentleman, Johnson respected the sanctity of her marriage to George Lanaux, with whom she had one child. He concealed his love for her until his death. But it is clear that she held some affection for him, too. During his final year, Johnson was gravely ill and needed help. He asked Marie to live in his home and care for him, and she agreed. It is not known if she brought her husband and child with her. Whatever relationship blossomed during his final months, Marie's companionship made Charles happy. As a final expression of his gratitude and affection, he named Marie his heir. She and her descendants lived in the mansion until 1953.

It seems possible that the many years he spent loving Marie from a distance may have something to do with the continued presence of Charles Johnson in the Lanaux Mansion. His interest in advising Ruth Bodenheimer on decorating and restoring the grandeur of the home may have risen from a desire to entice Marie to return from the grave. She may be there now, comforting the fastidious lawyer who was too much of a gentleman to reveal his love while he and Marie were alive.

MYSTERIOUS FRAGRANCE OF FLOWERS

Pitot House
1440 Moss Street
New Orleans 70119
504-482-0312
www.louisianalandmarks.org

The ghost that occupies this charming 1799 plantation home loves flowers. The sweet fragrance of jasmine, magnolias, roses, and azaleas is often detected in the master bedroom and dining room. Visitors often inquire about the potpourri, but Pitot House staff members deny using any decorative fragrance or cleaning agents with floral scents. On the other hand, it is known that at least one former resident had a passion for flowers.

Pitot House was named for James Pitot, who resided there from 1810 to 1819. He gained fame as the first American mayor of New Orleans, taking office in 1804. His administration was a whirlwind of activity. Under his leadership, a ferryboat service was started on the Mississippi, the police force was expanded with mounted patrols, a census was taken, streets were paved, and several civic building projects were started. He accomplished these things before he resigned in 1805 to devote his energies to managing his personal businesses.

A few years later, in 1810, Pitot purchased a two-story country home that stood on 30 acres outside the city on Bayou St. John. After a few happy years in the house, tragedy struck. On November 30, 1815, Pitot's wife, Marie-Jeanne, died giving birth to twin girls. Both girls followed their mother in death, one on December 23, 1815, and the other on January 22, 1816. If custom was followed, the house would have been filled with flowers on these sad occasions as funerals were staged within the home.

Pitot left the house in 1819. It passed through the hands of three owners until 1904, when Mother Francis Xavier Cabrini purchased it for the Missionary Sisters of the Sacred Heart of Jesus. It is said that Mother Cabrini had a passion for flowers and often walked throughout the neighborhood and nearby open spaces, gathering wild flowers and bouquets. The Missionary Sisters occupied the Pitot House until 1960, when it was deeded to the Louisiana Landmarks Society and moved a few hundred feet to make way for a new high school. Psychic investigations of the house have revealed a female spirit strongly attached to the master bedroom. This would have been the room in which Marie-Jeanne died and the room once occupied by Mother Cabrini.

Today, the Pitot House is operated by the Louisiana Landmarks Society. Furnished in early American and Louisiana antiques, the West Indies-style home gives visitors a taste of early-19th-century country life beyond the city limits of New Orleans.

THE GHOST DUELISTS

Dueling Oaks at New Orleans City Park
1 Palm Drive
New Orleans 70124-4608
504-482-4888
www.neworleanscitypark.com

In 18th-century New Orleans, an unwarranted intrusion, insulting comment, broken promise, or unfilled contract might have resulted in a Creole gentleman challenging the offender to a duel. The person challenged had only three options. He could publicly apologize and hope the offended gentleman would accept the apology. He could refuse the challenge, only to face a social stigma that would tarnish his family's reputation for generations and force him to leave town. Or he could accept the challenge and exercise his right to choose the weapon. Every Creole gentleman was trained in fencing—the blade arts—and the use of firearms.

The earliest duels were fought with swords. Many of these *affaires d'honneur* were conducted in St. Anthony's Garden behind St. Louis Cathedral. The ceremonies were quiet. The slamming of the blades against each other echoed off the walls of surrounding buildings and passed a short distance up the streets still gray with the early light of dawn. When pistols replaced swords as the dueling weapon of the day, however, things got noisy. The loud report of flint-lock pistols and the annoying sound of lead balls striking nearby doors, windows, and walls aroused complaints from the priests. They demanded the hot-headed Creoles take their disputes elsewhere. As a gesture to public safety, a stand of oaks at the end of Esplanade Avenue was designated the official dueling site.

It is unknown how many duels were fought at this location or at unofficial sites elsewhere, but it is believed to be more than 300. Many of these resulted in fatalities. Most often, the old saying, "pistols for

Several young men met their deaths under the ancient Dueling Oaks in City Park. Duels were fought here with swords and pistols.

two, brandy for one," rang true. Some of the wounded died days later of infections or organ damage. Many died on the spot and may have left something behind at the Dueling Oaks in City Park.

The aging dueling oaks stand between the New Orleans Museum of Art and Bayou Metairie. The trees aren't very tall, but their knotted limbs and thick, bent trunks reveal their 300 years. Under the shade of their limbs, sensitive ghost hunters have felt a rush of thick air, as if invisible bodies are moving about. At some spots, a sensation of profound sadness can be detected; perhaps indicating someone died there or someone fired a shot that killed a friend. Orbs have appeared on photographs and digital images taken under the oaks. The best time to capture orbs is early in the morning or at dusk. It may not be safe to visit this location after dark unless you are with others.

RESTLESS MADAM, JOSIE ARLINGTON

Metairie Cemetery
5100 Pontchartrain Boulevard
New Orleans 70124
504-486-6331

People have searched for the ghost of Josie Arlington at several locations. The feisty madam has been sought at a number of places— her grave site in Metairie Cemetery, on Esplanade Avenue at the former site of her mansion, the sidewalks that pass through the former red-light district known as Storyville, and locations in the French Quarter where the legendary madam stabled her girls and ran successful brothels. The search is bolstered by the suspicion that Arlington would not let a little thing like death separate her from her girls, her wealth, and her loyal clientele.

Having worked her way up from homelessness to considerable wealth, Arlington became a powerful woman in New Orleans with a book of secrets that could have destroyed the reputations of hundreds of the most important men in the state. Many believe she is still around, keeping watch over her tomb, her book of secrets, and the places she held dear.

Arlington, born Mamie Duebler around 1864, grew up in the Carrollton neighborhood of New Orleans. Her strict parents imposed every rule imaginable to keep their precious daughter away from sin and vice, but at the age of 17, Little Mary, as she was called, took up with gambler and pimp Philip "The Schwarz" Lobrano, who quickly corrupted her.

Arlington's legend starts with the night she came home long after curfew. Her irate parents locked the door and refused to let her in, thinking they would teach her a lesson by having her spend the night on the porch. But she kicked the door, pounded on the glass with her fists, and begged for admittance. When her stubborn father refused, Arlington screamed, awakening the entire neighborhood, then announced that she was leaving and would never return to the house. Later in life, she supported some of her relatives, but she never set foot in her Carrollton neighborhood again.

Arlington spent a night or two on the street before moving in with Lobrano, who immediately put her to work. Prostitution brought her easy money, but further removed the teenager from her upper-middle-class status. Until the day she died, Arlington longed for acceptance by the high society she and her girls served, but she was always denied. Even when she encountered her regular customers on the street, they would not acknowledge her in any way.

From age 17 to about 24, Arlington worked in some of the finest brothels of the city, becoming known for her good looks and fiery temper. By 1886, she'd realized that big money could be made by offering upscale girls and managing the business on her feet instead of on her back. While supporting Lobrano, Arlington opened her own brothel at 172 Customhouse Street (now Iberville) in the French Quarter. The place took on the temperament of its owner, however, and became the scene of several violent cat fights and a shooting in which Arlington's brother was wounded.

Faced with this notoriety, increasing competition, and lengthy appearances in court, Arlington closed her shop for a while. During this hiatus, she devised a new business plan and secured a stable of girls unknown to the city's regular johns. In 1896, she opened Chateau Lobrano d'Arlington at 215 Basin Street. This exotic establishment advertised a baroness from St. Petersburg and other ladies of

European royalty. By dressing the girls in expensive French lingerie and demanding that they keep their mouths shut, Arlington was able to conceal from the eager johns that their regal consorts were really from Baton Rouge and Biloxi. This marketing ploy made Arlington rich.

While catering to the peculiar lusts of the upper-crust New Orleans male society, Arlington also gathered a wealth of information that she used with tact to obtain legal favors, police protection, and other benefits. But her wealth, and the secrets she held, never gained her access to high society. Even when she purchased a mansion on fashionable Esplanade Avenue, residents of the neighborhood snubbed her.

Arlington died on Valentine's Day 1914 at the age of 50. While her funeral was sparsely attended, her grave site was filled with an ocean of flowers sent on behalf of customers, associates, and others who prayed that their secrets died with the famous madam.

Always denied access to the society that made her rich, Arlington got the last laugh when she purchased a grave site for $2,000 in Metairie Cemetery. She commissioned architect Albert Weiblen to build a massive tomb of polished marble and spared no expense in its construction. The tomb is topped with two urns from which carved flames tower above other monuments in the area. These flames evoke various interpretations of Arlington's intent. To some, they are the red lights of a brothel—traditional New Orleans flambeaux—indicating the madam's establishment is open and the girls are ready for business. To others, they are the flames of eternal life representing Arlington's refusal to give in to death.

Whatever the truth of the matter, these flames caused quite a stir when they were first unveiled. A nearby street lamp, swaying in the breeze, cast its flickering light on the carved stone creating the impression of four-foot-high flames. Huge crowds gathered to view the spectacle and confirm their wild speculations that death would not be the end of Josie Arlington. Brigades of police were summoned to control the crowds until the nearby street lamp was extinguished. For decades, the bizarre flames appeared on the anniversary of Arlington's death, even with the tomb shaded from the nearby street lamps by tall trees.

Another strange event at Arlington's tomb involves the statue that stands on the steps. The life-size bronze statue of a young lady in a Grecian gown carries a bouquet of roses in her left hand while she reaches for the doors of the tomb with her right hand. The maiden is believed to be a likeness of Arlington, reaching for the doors of society that were closed after she was locked out of her parent's home. Several mystical or paranormal events have been reported that involve the bronze statue. Two grave diggers—Todkins and Anthony—reported seeing a female figure come to life, step down from the tomb, and walk around the cemetery. According to their statements, they witnessed this event on two separate occasions. In fact, the statue was found elsewhere in the Metairie Cemetery, but it could have been moved by fraternity boys or other pranksters. Todkins and Anthony gave detailed reports of the statue's movements but they failed to report how much whiskey they had consumed prior to their sightings.

Several people have reported the sound of someone pounding on the huge bronze doors of the tomb, creating a noise heard by the cemetery's neighbors. This paranormal phenomenon may have something to do with the fact that Arlington's remains no longer rest inside her tomb.

Arlington left most of her wealth to her beloved niece and her business partner, John Brady. But she went to her grave unaware that the two were secret lovers. In fact, it is likely that Brady developed a relationship with the young lady knowing she would soon become wealthy. After Arlington's death, the two went on a spending spree that soon emptied the bank accounts. After selling the Arlington mansion for $35,000, their fun continued. But soon that money was gone, too. The last asset to be sold was Arlington's tomb.

One year and a day after Arlington's burial, her remains were removed and the tomb sold for a large sum. The new owner's name was carved on the marble walls, but that did not change the fact that this tomb belonged to Josie Arlington. Locals insist that the pounding that resonates throughout the cemetery on moonless nights is made by the ghost of the famous madam demanding access to her tomb.

Those who visit the tomb cannot help but notice something strange and prophetic about the statue. Josie could not have foretold

The tomb of notorious madam Josie Arlington in Metairie Cemetery now houses the remains of others, but her ghost still haunts the site.

the removal of her remains, yet the statue positioned on the steps, with outstretched hand and a bouquet of roses, certainly resembles a youthful Josie, seeking entry to her tomb just as she had sought entry to her father's house and to New Orleans' high society.

A partial apparition believed to be Josie Arlington has been spotted walking north on Esplanade Avenue, on the east side of the street, between Burgundy Street and St. Claude Avenue. She wears a black dress with full skirt and appears to be a full-figured woman. The apparition fades in and out at short intervals and appears to be looking at the grand houses that line the street.

If you visit Metairie Cemetery, Arlington's grave—now marked with the name J. A. Morales—can be found by entering the main gate on Pontchartrain Boulevard, turning left on Avenue H, then left again on Avenue G. Follow the road as it curves to the right but look to your left. You will see the tomb perched on a little hill surrounded by a heavy bronze chain.

SPIRITS OF THE OLD CEMETERY

St. Louis Cemetery No. 1
499 Basin Street
New Orleans 70112
504-482-5065

St. Louis Cemetery Number 1 opened in 1789, just in time to accommodate the large numbers of people killed by a disastrous fire, a hurricane, and recent epidemics of malaria, smallpox, and yellow fever. Thousands of poor people were buried in St. Louis Cemetery Number 1 in unmarked graves, many of them in mass graves. As the bodies disintegrated, the ground subsided. Wagonloads of soil were brought in almost daily to keep the ground at street level and provide new space for more bodies. Over many years, layers of dead bodies condensed and disintegrated, forming the white chalky dust that colors the ground to this day. As you walk around this cemetery, you are literally walking on the remains of thousands of the dead.

All of the cemeteries in New Orleans have legends and spooky stories about the dead and their monuments. Many of these stories arise

New Orleans' above-ground cemeteries—dubbed cities of the dead—house the dusty remains of the city's heroes, villains, and victims.

from the unique ways the dead were buried and honored in old New Orleans. In the early days of the French colony, attempts to bury the dead were disastrous. Bodies were buried in the highest ground available, which was the natural levee at the edge of the Mississippi River. During spring floods, erosion of the levee uncovered freshly buried corpses and bones of the long deceased, washing them through the streets and horrifying the town's citizens. By the mid-1700s, residents established cemeteries in the upper Quarter, but those cemeteries didn't fair much better. The high water table of the area caused freshly dug graves to fill with water. Caskets placed in the grave had to be weighted down with stones before they could be covered with earth. Mourners stood by, horrified at the gurgling sounds as water filled the casket, making a soggy corpse of the newly departed loved one.

By 1789, new cemeteries appeared, allowing for above-ground burial methods. St. Louis Cemetery Number 1 is a great example of the New Orleans style of burying the dead. Crypts and tombs stand several feet high, sometimes housing three or more bodies, one stacked on top of the other. The curious thing about these cities of the dead is that the bodies lasted only a short time. The ovenlike structures that housed the caskets cremated the corpses during the long, hot Louisiana summers. Instead of preserving the deceased, the tombs and climate turned them to dust.

By local tradition, one year and a day after burial, a grave could be opened and the casket removed. Ashes of the deceased were then placed in a *caveau* or vault built into the tomb's foundation. A recently deceased family member was then placed in the tomb or the spot was leased or sold to a stranger. It is not uncommon to see several unrelated names listed on the door of a tomb.

St. Louis Cemetery Number 1 was always known as a frightening place. City residents feared odors and wind-borne diseases that might arise from rotting dead bodies, and they feared the spirits of the dead. Older legends and stories are lost, but starting in the 1930s, cab drivers told bone-chilling stories about picking up people at the gates of the cemetery. After driving them to a specified destination, the drivers would find that the passengers had vanished from the back seat. These ghost passengers were said to appear lifelike and speak in a normal tone. One story, in particular, told of a woman dressed in a bridal gown who emerged from the cemetery's gate and hailed a cab, then gave an address in the Marigny. On reaching the destination, the woman disappeared. It is said that this event was repeated several times as the dead bride tried to return to her husband's home.

The ghost of voodoo priestess Marie Laveau is said to walk the narrow paths of this cemetery. Her tomb is one of the most visited monuments in New Orleans. Decorated with *X*s scratched on the stone work and offerings of money, candles, jewelry, bones, and flowers left by followers and the curious, Laveau's tomb generates a lot of ghostly legends. Enthralled visitors experience unexpected sensations ranging from cold spots to headaches and rapid breathing. Some people have reported seeing the priestess or feeling her touch. One man claimed he was slapped by an invisible hand while standing at her tomb cracking jokes about voodoo and the mysterious Marie Laveau. There are strange reports—from suspicious characters—of the tomb glowing with a green light and ghostly nude men and women dancing around it, celebrating a voodoo ritual.

The tomb of voodoo priestess Marie Laveau is among the most visited in New Orleans. Offerings that include bottles of rum, jewelry, and money are left untouched to avoid her wrath.

If you plan to visit this cemetery, you should join a tour group to take advantage of the knowledgeable guides. (See Appendix D.) They can point out graves of famous people that may be difficult for you to locate in the crowded maze of tombs. Also, many of the historic cemeteries in New Orleans can be unsafe. Touring with a group may provide essential security.

St. Louis Cemetery Number 2 is located three blocks away from Cemetery Number 1 on Claiborne Avenue. St. Louis Cemetery Number 3 is located on Esplanade Avenue near Bayou St. John.

THE ARMORY GHOST

Jackson Barracks Military Museum
6400 St. Claude Avenue
New Orleans 70146
504-278-8242
(Museum closed since Hurricane Katrina; check for reopening dates.)

First Sergeant Henry Brunig loved the horses that pulled the wagons and caissons of the Washington Artillery. When they were groomed and decked out in shiny harnesses, they looked magnificent, proudly marching before the heavy equipment. But in 1937, as the Washington Artillery became fully mechanized, the horses were no longer needed. Many of them were shipped off to other army camps, while 21 remained at Jackson Barracks, pronounced too old and unfit for military duty. In an expeditious move to get rid of the animals, the army executed them on the polo field. The gruesome event was too much for Sergeant Brunig. He had cared for them, watched them train, and as supply sergeant, had ordered every item from horseshoes to harnesses to keep them healthy and equipped for duty. The day after the execution, Brunig stood in the center of the barracks warehouse and shot himself.

Thirty-two years later, the army built an armory on the site of the horses' execution. Not long after the building opened, Sergeant Brunig resumed his duties. For the past 30 years, members of the 141st Battalion, Washington Artillery, have heard some strange sounds in the big building. While working late at night, army personnel hear doors slamming, toilets flushing, and water running. Sergeant Brunig may be checking out the new facility, looking for items that may need to be replaced. Others, including civilian workers and visitors, have heard disembodied footsteps. These strange sounds have occurred many times when only one or two people were in the building, leading to the widely held belief that a ghost walks the building.

Jackson Barracks was founded in 1833 as part of a security system intended to protect New Orleans from invasion by way of the Mississippi River. It stands on high ground not far from the river's edge. Modern roads and construction obscure the view of the Mississippi. In 1866, the barracks was named in honor of the hero of New Orleans, General Andrew Jackson. Several famous military commanders have visited the barracks or spent time there on official duty. The list includes Robert E. Lee and Ulysses S. Grant, both stationed there as lieutenants in 1844-45; Confederate general P.G.T. Beauregard; Union general George B. McClellan; and World War I general John J. "Black Jack" Pershing. Thousands of others, unknown to history, have also served here before moving on to less hospitable posts. Today, Jackson Barracks is home to the Louisiana Army and Air National Guard headquarters. It also contains a fascinating military museum complete with tanks, aircraft, and artillery.

In the 1870s, members of the 7th Calvary, Custer's brigade, trained there before heading north to meet the Sioux at Little Big Horn on June 22, 1876. Four of Custer's men, George W. Williams, Patrick Duran, Henderson Lewis, and John Coughlan, died at the barracks of yellow fever in 1875. The men were buried on the grounds and the graves marked with regulation army headstones. For unknown reasons, the army moved the bodies in 1883 to a military cemetery in Indiana, but neglected to relocate the headstones for Williams, Duran, Lewis, and Coughlan. Today, the four headstones are on display in the Jackson Barracks Military Museum. Psychic investigation suggests that the ghost of one of the four dead soldiers has stayed behind with his headstone. An intense cold spot can be detected hovering over the monument that belongs to Henderson Lewis. Orbs have been captured on film and in digital images. Sensitive people who touch the monuments get the feeling that there is something different about Lewis's headstone. Ghost hunters might get some interesting findings with electromagnetic field detectors and

The ghost of First Sergeant Henry Brunig haunts Jackson Barracks, where Robert E. Lee and Ulysses S. Grant were once stationed before the Civil War.

recorders that can capture electronic voice phenomena. The museum is housed in a brick building well over 100 years old. It is quiet, with subdued light, and seldom crowded.

Talk to museum docents and facility caretakers about other legends of Jackson Barracks. There are rumors that night staff members have seen the ghosts of several soldiers walking about the place.

HEROES AND THE DEFEATED ENEMY

Chalmette Battlefield
Jean Lafitte National Historic Park and Preserve
8606 West St. Bernard Highway
Chalmette 70043
504-281-0510

The soldiers who fought at Chalmette Battlefield were a lot like the young country they defended. General Andrew Jackson's forces included U.S. Army regular units, the New Orleans militia, a large number of former Haitian slaves who were free men of color, frontiersmen from Tennessee, Kentucky, and Missouri, and a contingent of pirates led by Jean Lafitte. These 4,000 troops banded together to repel the British invasion, with only eight killed and 13 wounded. The hapless British lost 2,000 men, and several hundred were captured. The death of so many in such a short period of time on such a small battlefield has left environmental imprints that sensitive ghost hunters may detect.

Still reveling over their successful invasion of Washington, D.C., the British attempted a strike at the underbelly of America to seize control of the Mississippi River. New Orleans stood as the key to controlling commerce on the river and halting economic support of American military operations in the north. With a flotilla of more than 50 ships and 10,000 experienced troops, General Edward Pakenham landed his forces at Lake Borgne in December 1814 and began the march through the cypress swamps to the Crescent City.

When word of the British advance reached Jackson, the charismatic leader rallied the city, bringing together combatants who would otherwise have nothing to do with each other. Thieves, pirates, and buckskin-clad frontiersmen fought side by side with regular army men. Even New Orleans dandies showed up with fancy weapons and polished boots. In two days, they erected a three-fifths-mile-long mud rampart on the edge of dry Rodriguez Canal on the Chalmette Plantation. The canal formed a ditch that would put the British in an extremely vulnerable position if they tried to scale the rampart.

With the arrival of fresh troops in the early days of January 1815, the British staged skirmishes on the east bank of the Mississippi and moved artillery onto Chalmette Plantation. On the morning of January 8, the British advanced across the field, and American gunboats opened fire.

Within two hours, General Pakenham and two of his senior generals were dead along with most of the Scottish Highland Brigade. One of Pakenham's officers took command, but wisely disobeyed Pakenham's dying order to continue the attack. As the British withdrew, they left 2,000 men dead on the field and several hundred held captive by the rag-tag Americans.

Today, the Rodriguez Canal and ramparts remain on Chalmette

Battlefield, marking the place of a great American victory. You can walk the grounds and visit the spots where General Pakenham died, the Scottish Highlanders were killed in their foolish diagonal march across the field, the British left-column attack was cut down by cannon fire from Lafitte's pirates, or hundreds died in hand-to-hand combat in the canal. At these spots, sensitive ghost hunters sometimes feel a thickened atmosphere or cold spots that may represent residual emotions from the battle. Walking the ramparts, sensitive people may also feel a pulling sensation as if gravity has increased many times. These spots are the likely locations at which several soldiers died.

The broad expanse of the grass-covered battlefield offers opportunities for solitary wandering away from other visitors. Some people sit on the grass and use meditation to increase their sensitivity to both environmental imprints and residual emotions from the battle.

Ghosts of British invaders and American defenders of New Orleans haunt Chalmette Battlefield, where the final battle of the War of 1812 took place.

GHOSTS OF THE PLANTATION FAMILY

Woodland Plantation Bed-and-Breakfast Inn
21997 Highway 23
West Point a la Hache 70083
1-800-231-1514
www.woodlandplantation.com

The recent history of Woodland Plantation is a familiar one. Nearly in ruins, the 150-year-old plantation was purchased in the 1990s by people who didn't truly comprehend the monumental tasks they would face to restore the building and grounds. During the first months of work, the house was occupied by a solitary person who heard strange sounds. Later, apparitions appeared. Investigations into the plantation's past revealed a dark history and plenty of reasons for spirits of the dead to remain. They also revealed why Woodland Plantation, after its renovation and rebirth, is a beautiful and popular country inn.

Woodland Plantation was built in 1834 by William Johnson, one of the first chief pilots on the Mississippi River. Captain Johnson came to the lower Mississippi from Nova Scotia in the 1790s, possibly to escape his reputation as a pirate and scoundrel. With partner George Bradish, a fellow Canadian with a similar history, Johnson established legitimate businesses while engaging in the illegal slave trade, sometimes in association with pirate Jean Lafitte.

Johnson's 4,000-square-foot Creole cottage, surrounded by 11,000 acres of sugarcane fields, passed to his son, Bradish Johnson, in 1857. The plantation was one of the few to remain prosperous after the Civil War, but it eventually declined and the buildings fell into disrepair. The Prohibition era of the 1920s brought new prosperity. Situated at the mouth of the Mississippi River, the plantation was a haven for bootleggers who rented space to store contraband. By the 1940s, most of the 11,000 acres had been sold, and the house sat desolate, surrounded by overgrown trees and shrubs. The remains of unusual brick slave quarters sat nearby, concealed by tall grass. The four two-story structures were more like jails than dormitories. Iron rings embedded in the walls anchored the heavy chains that imprisoned slaves until they could be illegally sold or they died. The buildings were destroyed by Hurricane Betsy in 1965.

When Foster Creppel and his parents, Jacques and Claire, bought the old plantation in 1997 by auction, the house did not appear worth saving. All the windows were broken, doors were missing, owls and other winged creatures lived on the second floor, rats and other rodents were everywhere, and alligators and snakes inhabited the spaces beneath the main floor.

Much of the ghostly activity discovered at Woodland Plantation is attributed to Bradish Johnson. This stylish gentleman dressed in striped pants, Prince Albert coats, and silk hats. His favorite accessory was a gold-tipped cane, which produced a loud tap as he strode across the wide rooms and galleries of his home.

Foster Creppel began his restoration of the dilapidated house by moving in and becoming its solitary living resident. During the first three months, nights brought him little rest from his labors due to the persistent pounding on the floorboards of the second story. Often resembling heavy footsteps, a loud tapping sound was also heard, as if someone were hitting the floor with a heavy stick or cane. At times, the footfalls were so numerous that Creppel thought several people were walking the second floor. Exasperated from a lack of sleep, Creppel proclaimed, "If you wake me up one more time I am going to burn this whole house down."

From that night on, the ghosts of Woodland have remained quiet but still inquisitive and playful. Investigators believe the ghosts of Bradish Johnson and members of his large family wander the house at night checking on Creppel's renovations. Some of these ghosts were seen by visitor Richard Fern. Fern awoke in the middle of the night to find a young boy standing at the foot of his bed. When questioned, the apparition faded away. Others have detected a female presence believed to be Bradish's mother, Sarah. The pale apparitions of two women standing with a man have been seen on the first floor. Some visitors feel a cold breeze or the odd sensation of someone standing behind them.

The site of the slave quarters is now occupied by Spirits Hall, the former 1883 St. Patrick's Church, which was partially disassembled and moved to Woodland Plantation in 1999. The building was magnificently restored and is used for parties, weddings, and banquets. Ghost hunters believe former parishioners may roam the old building. Also, the spirits of slaves who languished in the old quarters while chained to the brick walls may be detected there. Ghost hunters should also investigate the ruins of the sugar mill and the overseer's cabin.

GHOST SENTRIES OF FORT PIKE

Fort Pike State Historic Site
27100 Chef Menteur Highway
New Orleans 70129
504-662-5703
(Closed since Hurricane Katrina; check for reopening dates.)

Fort Pike stands guard over the Rigolets, a narrow passage between the Gulf of Mexico and Lake Pontchartrain. Its location, 23 miles from central New Orleans, was strategic during the British attempt to invade the city in 1814-15. Following the War of 1812, President James Monroe ordered construction of a series of forts along the entire Atlantic and Gulf coasts as a deterrent to any other foreign invasion. These fortifications were placed at key points, guarding cities, ports, navigable rivers, and bays where troops might land. Four installations were constructed for the protection of New Orleans— Forts Jackson and St. Philip on the Mississippi, Fort Livingston on Barataria Bay, and Fort Pike at the Rigolets.

Named for explorer Zebulon Montgomery Pike (1779-1813), for whom Pike's Peak was also named, the brick and masonry fort was constructed in 1816 with major renovations in the 1850s and 1867. It was designed to withstand attack from sea and land, with two protective moats and a garrison of up to 400 men. At the outbreak of the Civil War, the Louisiana militia captured the fort with little resistance from federal troops. Confederates occupied the fort until 1862, when Union forces took control of New Orleans. By the end of the Civil War, development of more effective artillery made the fort obsolete. By 1871, it was under the care of a single ordnance sergeant and remained so until the U.S. Army abandoned the fort in 1890.

The name of the solitary ordnance sergeant assigned to watch over Fort Pike from 1871 to 1890 is not known, but he remains dedicated to his duty. Long after his death, the man is still on watch. Visitors who walk the cool, dark casemates, or gun chambers, often feel that someone is following close behind. On turning around, they are surprised to find no one there. If you can find a quiet spot, stand there for a while. You may hear the disembodied sound of a pair of boots walking on the masonry floor.

On the barbette tier—an exposed upper level—several smoothbore cannons used to sit at the stone emplacements. At some of these emplacements, people have detected cold spots, and some have heard the sound of boots scuffing on the stone and masonry. Psychic investigation has revealed a lonely spirit, dedicated to duty, who seems pleased to have visitors at the fort.

Ghost hunters, especially those who use psychic methods for investigation, may find other spirits trapped at Fort Pike. During the Seminole Wars in the 1830s, the fort was used as a prison for hundreds of Seminole Indians and their black slaves. These prisoners were kept there for long periods of time before being relocated to Oklahoma. It is certain that some of these unfortunate souls died at Fort Pike of wounds, infections related to their incarceration, or chronic illness.

Prisoners were housed in some of the casemates after removal of the cannons. Up to 253 prisoners were crammed into the spaces, making it easier for the small number of troops to guard them. The close feeling often experienced there may be the spirit of one of these prisoners seeking attention from 21st-century visitors.

CHAPTER 6

Upriver from New Orleans

There are many popular destinations for day trips or weekend get-aways within two hours' driving time of New Orleans. Many of these locations, such as the historic buildings and ships of Baton Rouge and the plantation houses on the old River Road, have a rich historical legacy. They offer fascinating glimpses of the French colonial period, old American South, Civil War era, and the emergence of the New South.

Before the Civil War, both banks of the Mississippi between New Orleans and Baton Rouge were occupied by large plantations anchored by huge manor houses. Most of them spanned only a few hundred yards of riverfront, but extended inland as much as a mile. These plantations were the economic engines of the region and the seats of social and political institutions. Many of these plantations are now museums, restaurants, or inns. They are great places for ghost hunters to experience the Southern ghosts described in this chapter.

Check with a local visitor's bureau or historical society to get a map of the area and information about special events, tours, festivals, and anniversaries of historical importance.

THE RESTLESS DESTREHANS

Destrehan Plantation
13034 River Road
Destrehan 70047
985-764-9315
www.destrehanplantation.org

For more than a century it was rumored that the pirate Jean Lafitte haunted Destrehan Plantation, the queen of the lower Mississippi valley. According to legend, he secretly and illegally sold slaves and stolen jewels throughout the region and had many business dealings with at least one member of the Destrehan family. It is said that Lafitte, being on good terms with this wealthy family, was often a guest in their home. During these visits, he is said to have managed to bury some of his treasure there. After the Civil War, stories began to circulate that Lafitte had close ties to the wealthy Destrehans. This inspired local treasure hunters—most of them former pirates or sons of pirates—to roam about the plantation searching for anything of value. Some of these scoundrels started stories about Lafitte's ghost as a tactic to scare away competitors. It was said that the pirate was surrounded by a fierce band of followers armed to the teeth and eager to spill blood. The story evolved to include the tale that inside the house, Lafitte's ghost appeared to those he deemed worthy and pointed to the locations of his hidden loot.

In the early 1900s, the house sat vacant for 12 years. During this period, treasure hunters and vandals entered the property searching for the pirate's gold. They tore the plaster from the walls, ripped out marble fireplaces, chopped holes in the floors, and stole anything of value. The once magnificent Destrehan mansion was nearly in ruins, all because of rumors of a pirate's ghost and hidden treasure.

Fortunately, the grand mansion was saved from further destruction and ultimately restored to its former glory. Stories about Lafitte's ghost have persisted to this day, however. His appearances, it is reported, are limited to the kitchen, where he points to the hearth. By the 1980s, reports of Lafitte's ghost were infrequent, at best, while other hauntings were noticed by workmen. During major restorations, disembodied footsteps were heard in some of the rooms. An article in the *New Orleans Times-Picayune,* dated November 1, 1980, reported that several workmen heard footsteps and often saw a tall, thin man. The gentleman was dressed in dark clothing from the antebellum period and remained visible for only a few seconds. This ghost has been seen standing on the porch by plantation staff and visitors, looking through in the windows. He looked so real that staff members have gone to the door, thinking a visitor had arrived. When they opened the door, they found the porch vacant. It is believed that this gentleman is the ghost of a former owner, Jean Noel D'Estrehan. (The spelling of Jean Noel's surname has been anglicized to Destrehan.)

Visitors touring the home have encountered D'Estrehan. He appears lifelike, giving the impression that he is a costumed docent following visitors through the house. Some visitors claim that he has spoken to them and responded to their questions.

Jean Noel D'Estrehan purchased the mansion in 1802 from its original owner, Antoine Robert de Longy. He made several improvements to the house and changed the plantation crop from indigo to sugar, quickly creating vast wealth. Jean Noel died in 1823. His wife, Claudine Eleanor Celeste de Longy, daughter of the original owner, followed him in death a year later. Part ownership of the plantation passed to Stephen Henderson after he married their daughter Eleonore "Zelia" D'Estrehan.

It was during Henderson's ownership that Jean Lafitte might have conducted business on the plantation. One argument against this speculation is that Henderson resided in New Orleans and spent little time on the plantation. Eleonore's brother, Nicholas Noel D'Estrehan, lived on the property for years while his plantation, on the west bank of the Mississippi, was under construction. It is believed that this young man was an admirer of the charismatic outlaw and welcomed him to Destrehan, as well as his own plantation. In fact, Lafitte may have used a canal on Nicholas's property to conduct his business and escape from local police.

The ghost of Nicholas Noel D'Estrehan has been identified as roaming his father's plantation. This identification was made through an accident that occurred in 1826. While inspecting the sugar mill on the property, Nicholas's arm became entangled in the machinery. He saved himself by cutting off the mutilated limb. After that, he wore a cape, even on the warmest of days, to preserve his gentlemanly appearance. Many people have seen a man with a cape draped over his shoulders walking the upper galleries and entrance foyer. Details of his apparition are so clear that witnesses have noticed he is missing his right arm.

There is speculation that the ghost of Eleonore "Zelia" D'Estrehan has taken up residence in her childhood home as well. After their wedding,

The ghost of pirate Jean Lafitte has been spotted at Destrehan Plantation, directing living souls to the location of his legendary hidden treasure.

Eleonore and Stephen Henderson lived in New Orleans, seldom visiting the plantation that Eleonore loved as a child. In 1830, while in New York to amend her will, she died mysteriously in her hotel room. Eleonore had wished to leave her share of the huge estate to her sister, Louise Odile, maintaining at least part ownership in the D'Estrehan bloodline. With her death, Henderson became the sole owner of the estate.

GHOST OF HITLER'S HORSE

La Branche Plantation Dependency House
11244 River Road
Saint Rose 70087
504-468-8843

At the end of World War II, Adolf Hitler's horse, Nordlicht, was transported to the United State as a spoil of war. The horse was kept by the army until 1948, when it was purchased by Dr. S. Walter Mattingly and moved to La Branche Plantation. Nordlicht remained on the plantation for 20 years, siring several offspring. When he died, he was buried near the pastures he had roamed and a marker was erected. The horse's remains stayed at rest in the pasture until sometime in the 1980s, when gardeners uncovered his bones. The grave was immediately restored, but the accidental desecration awoke old Nordlicht. From that time on, the ghost horse has been a common site around the old plantation.

Lisa Lentini, director of the plantation grounds, spotted a horse in the corral late one day. She assumed the animal was one of her sister's horses. Knowing that animals should not be left outside the barn at night, Lentini entered the corral, touched the horse on the nose, and spoke to it. She told the horse he should get back in the barn. The lively animal turned and ran into the barn, then vanished. When Lentini checked the barn, she found all the horses in their stalls with the gates locked. The horse she had seen in the corral was not among them. Visitors and several family members who live on the plantation have also seen the brown horse with the white spotted nose. He gallops a short distance and then disappears.

The historic La Branche Plantation, built in 1790, including the dependency house and slave quarters, invites speculation that ghosts reside there. The plantation house was burned during the Civil War, probably as a result of shots fired from Union gunboats on the river. Some believe the La Branche family burned the grand house rather than see it confiscated by the invading Yankees. Today, only the ruins stand amid grass and trees.

The dependency house, built in 1792 by owner Alexandre La Branche, still stands and is open to visitors. Dependencies were buildings set apart from manor houses that provided functions vital to maintaining the households. Usually, they contained a kitchen, laundry, or sleeping quarters for adolescent males. After the age of 14, the sons of plantation masters were considered old enough to carry on an independent lifestyle and come and go as they pleased. Having a residence close to the manor house assured the sons' presence at meals and important family gatherings, but also gave them the independence needed to become men at an early age.

The ghost of Adolf Hitler's horse has been seen at La Branche Plantation. The ghosts of humans still occupy the 1792 dependency that housed servants.

The La Branche Dependency House is haunted by spirits of people who resided within its thick walls. The fragrance of strong perfume has been detected by several visitors outside the building, on the galleries, and inside the four rooms. This might indicate a visit by the lady of the manor, Suzanne La Branche, to check on her sons. Inside, people have seen candlesticks fly off the mantle and a rocking chair moving with an invisible occupant. Several sensitive visitors have heard the faint cry of a baby. In 1920, a young woman rented one of the rooms and gave birth to twins. One of the babies died within a few days. The muffled cries could indicate the ghostly presence of this baby.

In the slave quarters, ghostly activity includes the odors of pungent cigar smoke, strong perfume, and a sumptuous meal on the stove. The latter two fragrances often occur together, suggesting the master and mistress of the plantation—probably Jean Baptise and Suzanne La Branche—are taking an evening stroll around their plantation, making certain all is quiet at the slave quarters.

A REBEL'S CURSE AND THREE DEAD MASTERS

Ormond Plantation
13786 River Road
Destrehan 70047
985-764-8544
www.plantation.com

Ormond Plantation is an inviting, pleasant place with a history that fascinates its guests. As a popular bed-and-breakfast inn, the beautiful grounds and historic manor house offer a peaceful ambience that reveals some of the grace and charm of life in the Old South. But it was not always this way. About ten years after the house was constructed in the late 1780s by Pierre d'Trepagnier, a slave uprising took place. The leader of the rebellion was captured and punished severely. While he was tied to a tree and whipped, he is said to have cast a spell on his master and the plantation. Legend says that the slave's curse invoked an early death for masters of Ormond Plantation.

It didn't take long for the curse to strike the first victim. One night, while Pierre d'Trepagnier was enjoying dinner with his family, a servant entered the dining room and announced that a royal Spanish carriage had arrived. The servant explained that a gentleman seated in the carriage wished to have a word with the master. d'Trepagnier stepped out of the house and into the carriage. In a moment, it sped away into the night, and d'Trepagnier was never heard from again. The Spanish government—Louisiana was a part of the Spanish colony in 1798—denied sending an envoy to Ormond Plantation. As days and weeks passed, it became clear that d'Trepagnier was not coming home.

By 1819, the plantation had been sold twice. From 1805 to 1819 it was owned by Colonel Richard Butler. Fearing the yellow-fever epidemic that ravaged all of Louisiana, Butler sold Ormond to his brother-in-law and moved to Bay St. Louis, Mississippi. But this move did not stop the slave's curse. In 1820, Butler and his wife died of the fever. He was 43 years old.

The curse did not surface again until 1898, when the property was owned by state senator Basile LaPlace. A vocal adversary of the Ku Klux Klan, LaPlace was accustomed to taking precautions when he traveled. While at home, though, he relied on his staff of servants, dogs, and Ormond's isolation for protection. But, like d'Trepagnier, LaPlace was called from the dinner table one night to receive a gentleman at the door who wished to give the senator important information. Everyone assumed this odd meeting had run late, so they retired before the estate's master had returned to the house. In the morning, they found his bullet-riddled body hanging from a tall oak tree near the entrance to the plantation.

Subsequent owners escaped the curse, but hauntings began as early as 1880. On a moonless night, a servant who was sent down to the river to meet a steamboat encountered something strange and frightening that many believe is still present around the grounds of the old plantation. As the servant walked the familiar path back to the house, he ran into something large, darker than the night, and menacing. As the servant moved, the black object followed him. Panicked, the servant ran to the house screaming that he had been attacked by a ghost. Later that night, a strong wind rose from the river and battered the windows and doors of Ormond. A gentleman seated in the parlor watched, in amazement, as black smoke entered the room through a key hole. In moments, the smoke took the shape of a tall man and filled the room with gloom and anger. Stunned by the vision, the man tried to cry out, but froze as a cold, bony hand touched his face.

Could this dark, menacing ghost be one of Ormond's former masters or the angry spirit of the rebellious slave? Recent visitors to Ormond Plantation have not reported such unpleasant experiences, but sensitive ghost hunters who walk the grounds just after sunrise or late at night may feel the shadowy presence first described in 1880. Staff members of the Ormond Bed & Breakfast often see a man dressed in dark, 19th-century clothing wandering the grounds behind the manor house. When spotted, he does not create the same frightening atmosphere as the large, dark entity that roamed the front of the estate near the river.

In the driveway at the front of the house, I detected a haunting—probably an environmental imprint—of a carriage coming to a stop. The sounds of straining leather and horse's hooves were remarkably clear. In addition, some of the staff members at Ormond Plantation believe that a young woman haunts one of the rooms on the upper floor. Her face has been seen looking out the window toward the river. She may be one of Pierre d'Trepagnier's daughters, awaiting the return of her papa.

SAN FRANCISCO ON THE MISSISSIPPI

San Francisco Plantation
2646 River Road
Garyville 70051-0950
www.sanfranciscoplantation.org

Charles Marmillion was born into a world of wealth and privilege, but he was no stranger to tragedy. In 1856, at the age of 16, he lost his father, Edmond Bozonier Marmillion. His passing was made even sadder, as the patriarch had only recently completed construction of a grand mansion on the river, Marmillion Plantation. His dreams of a happy, growing family flourishing within the spectacular 11,000-square-foot house died with him.

Charles had barely attained manhood when he was pressed into service during the Civil War. Working his way up through the ranks, he became a captain in the Confederate army and fought in four major battles, including Gettysburg. He was captured and escaped, only to be captured again and imprisoned for two years. Sometime during the war, his legs were injured. After the war, he returned home, taking up residence with his brother, Valsin, and Valsin's German wife, Louise, in the grand mansion their father had built.

Valsin renamed the plantation after Louise nearly bankrupted him with remodeling costs. He told his friends he was *sans fruschin*, meaning "without a penny in my pocket." Over the years, people in the region altered the phrase to St. Frusquin. When the property was purchased in 1879 by Achille D. Bourgère, the name was changed to San Francisco.

Charles and his brother saved the plantation from a post-war economy that ruined many plantations along the river. By 1870, they had achieved some success in the sugar business, and the future of the plantation appeared to be assured. But in 1871, Valsin died at the age of 44. Charles did his best to carry on the business with Louise and helped care for his brother's three young daughters. Chronic pain and weakness in his legs, as well as some kind of lung disease, possibly due to his habit of smoking cigars, disabled him to a great extent and contributed to his death in 1875 at the age of 35.

Realizing that she could not maintain the plantation without Charles, Louise Marmillion sold the 1,500-acre estate in 1879 and returned to her native Germany with her three daughters. She left behind two other daughters, who died before the age of two, in graves covered with flowers. One of the girls died after falling down the stairs.

With this long history of struggling against monumental events and premature deaths, it is no wonder that the ghost of Charles Marmillion still roams his beloved home. Ghost hunters and psychics working with the ISPR verified his presence. They encountered a

The ghost of Charles Marmillion roams his estate, San Francisco Plantation, on River Road, leaving the odor of cigar smoke in the air.

man in his mid-30s who smoked cigars and suffered from a chronic respiratory illness. This entity wore a long coat and had reddish-brown hair and a mustache. Their description matched photographs of Charles Marmillion. He was desperately ill, coughing, and saddened that Sans Fruschin would be left without a Marmillion to keep his father's dream alive. This ghost was found in Charles's main-floor office, in one of the bedrooms, and in the dining room. My recent visit produced similar impressions. I detected a male presence in the bedroom.

Other ghosts have been seen at this plantation house. Some people have spotted two little girls dressed in white, playing under the trees and having tea parties on the lawn. It is believed that they are the daughters of Valsin and Louise Marmillion. In a second-floor bedroom, the ghost of a little girl has been found suffering from a serious illness. Sensitive ghost hunters have encountered a second male presence there, as well as on the first floor. This may be Edmond Bozonier Marmillion enjoying the comforts of the house that was completed only days before his death.

OAK ALLEY GHOSTS

Oak Alley Plantation
3645 Louisiana Highway 18 (Great River Road)
Vacherie 70090
225-265-2151
www.oakalleyplantation.com

Four ghosts have been spotted at magnificent Oak Alley Plantation. Three of them are believed to be members of the illustrious family that built this plantation, which still evokes romantic notions of the Old South and images of *Gone With the Wind*.

The oak trees that promoted riverboat captains to call the Bon Sejour plantation "Oak Alley" were planted in the very early 1700s. Capuchin monks, passing by the property in 1722, mentioned the impressive twin rows of trees in their journals. The two rows of 14 oaks, planted 80 feet apart, form a driveway that spans the 800 feet from River Road to the manor house. For more than 300 years, the trees have survived floods and hurricanes to form a natural canopy that makes the house appear to be a mystical place at the end of a long and enchanting tunnel.

Jacques Telesphore Roman, and his wife, Celina, bought the property in 1836, razed the small cottage that stood at the head of the oak alley, and erected the classical revival house that stands today. In spite of the beauty of the place and Celina's privileged life on a successful sugar plantation, she longed for the society of New Orleans. Jacques preferred to stay home and enjoy the peaceful ambience of the great house. Also, during the ten years he lived in the house, his health had declined. He died in 1848, leaving Celina to manage the property. Always deep in mourning, she left the business affairs of the plantation to an overseer and made frequent trips to New Orleans to escape the unpleasant memories of Jacques's slow death. With the wave of destruction that came with the Civil War, Oak Alley fell upon hard times. Celina sold the property in 1866 for $32,800. After her death, she seems to have returned to the house she had shared with her beloved Jacques.

The ghost of Celina Roman has been seen in daylight among the famed oak trees and in several spots throughout the main house. She is dressed in her black mourning clothes, including a veil that hangs nearly to her waist. Unlike most apparitions, this ghost appears to be a living person. She has been mistaken for one of the tour guides who dress in period costume. When she vanishes before the eyes of admiring visitors, gasps of astonishment tell you someone has seen Celina Roman. Jacques Telesphore Roman has also been seen in broad daylight. Ghost hunters, plantation staff, and visitors who gaze out the first-floor windows are often surprised to see the plantation's original owner looking back at them.

The sad ghost of Louise Roman, daughter of Celina and Jacques, has been seen in the staff's break room, the overseer's room, and the entry hall. Louise lost her leg in an unfortunate accident while dashing up the stairs and spent a reclusive life in the big house. Years later when she died, she was buried with the portion of her leg that was amputated in her youth. That may explain why this ghost appears intact, completely lifelike, with clearly discernible features. She, too, is dressed in black, mourning her father or the loss of an exceptional life that was the birthright of every daughter of a rich planter. When Louise appears, sensitive witnesses are filled with sadness and despair.

On the second floor, the ghost of a young girl is seen as she walks about in a blue and white nightgown. Witnesses report that she has auburn hair hanging to her shoulders and appears lifelike. Psychic investigation of this ghost has revealed that she is 12 years old and died in the house. She may have been the daughter of one of the many owners between 1866 and 1912, when the house was abandoned.

Paranormal activity, attributed to other ghosts at Oak Alley, has been reported by overnight guests and day visitors. This includes the sounds of a carriage arriving at the front of the manor house, complete with rattling chain, straining leather, and neighing horses. On the second floor, an empty rocking chair moves as if it is occupied by an unseen spirit. The odor of tobacco and the fragrance of roses have been reported when none of these were in the house. In the upstairs sick room and nursery, visitors have felt intense cold spots. Also in

Ghosts of the Roman family still occupy their plantation home, Oak Alley. Some of them have been seen walking the famous oak alley, which was planted in the early 1700s.

these locations, people experience burning sensations on their arms and foreheads, as if they had spiked a fever. In the oak alley, the ghost of Celina Roman has been spotted as she wanders among the trees. Cold spots and thickened air, about the dimensions of a man, have also been encountered at several locations along the 800-foot driveway.

If you visit Oak Alley, stop at nearby Laura Plantation at 2247 Louisiana 18 in Vacherie. In the spring of 2005, the house was in the final stages of a major renovation. After it opened in 2006, it quickly became a good place for ghost hunting. Often spirits become active after remodeling, renovation, or rebuilding. They come for a visit to see what has been done to their beloved homes.

You should also stop at the site of one of the most beautiful and extravagant plantations of the region. It is marked by a small sign alongside the road. The place was known as Le Petit Versailles, home of Valcour Frances Gabriel Aime. The house, gardens, zoo, stables, fish ponds, and all of its outbuildings deteriorated after most of Valcour's family died. The great house was destroyed by fire in 1920. Today, only fields and clumps of trees remain. But some believe Valcour's ghost wanders the grounds, searching for his home and the jewels and money—valued at two million dollars in 1862—that he hid from invading Union soldiers.

GHOSTS OF THE SLAVE VILLAGE

Laurel Valley Village
595 Louisiana Highway 308
Thibodaux 70301
985-447-2902

Laurel Valley Plantation is a working farm not open to visitors. But you can turn off Louisiana 308 and drive 1.25 miles on unimproved road to view the largest slave village still standing in the United States. Ghost hunters traveling east from Thibodaux should be prepared to turn left after passing the Laurel Valley Store Museum. Look for antique trains on display near this intersection to find the unnamed road leading to the slave village.

The village is composed of more than 65 structures, mostly duplex houses with a fireplace and chimney at each end. Built of wood, these fascinating houses have withstood the challenging climate of south Louisiana for more than 150 years. Most of them have a porch running the length of the house. Scattered about the village are outhouses, barns, a school, and sheds. These former homes of slaves look quite forlorn with missing doors, crumbling brick work, and sagging roofs. The atmosphere is chilling even on a warm day. Creepy feelings surround sensitive visitors and evoke a sense of sadness. It is likely that many slaves who labored here were born in these shacks and never traveled beyond the boundaries of the plantation. It is clear that many slaves died here.

A fence prevents ghost hunters from entering these structures—they are not structurally sound enough for touring—but when standing a short distance from a shack and looking through the gaping

More than 60 structures comprise the slave village at Laura Valley Plantation in Thibodaux, southwest of New Orleans.

doorway at a crumbling hearth, you can detect the strong environmental imprints. Ghost hunters have detected the aroma of food being cooked and smoke from the fireplaces. Slamming doors, the muted call of a man with a strong voice, laughing children, and creaking floorboards have all been heard when no one is present but the ghost hunter. Some visitors have seen partial apparitions of male and female slaves walking among the houses as they head for the fields. Apparitions of women and children have been seen standing on the porches or sitting on the steps as well.

Even if ghostly activity is not detected, this historic slave village is worth visiting. For modern visitors, it is impossible to imagine the life of a slave. But sensitive people who walk among these structures feel the thickened atmosphere dripping with profound sadness.

GUARDIAN OF THE CEMETERY

Madewood Plantation
4250 Louisiana 308
Napoleonville 70390
800-375-7151
www.madewood.com

Behind this massive 1840s plantation manor house is a graveyard that contains the remains of the estate's first owner, Colonel Thomas Pugh, his family, and descendents. The graveyard has all the classic elements to make this a very spooky place after sunset. A 300-year-old oak tree spreads huge limbs outward, shading the headstones and casting long, eerie shadows at dusk. The cast-iron fence and gate with creaking hinges adds a feeling of foreboding as visitors enter the place.

Tall, ornate monuments and large slabs of concrete covering the graves contain the long-deceased Pugh family. Colonel Thomas Pugh engaged the services of famed architect Henry Howard to build the Greek Revival-style manor house between 1840 and 1848. Standing resplendent on Pugh's 10,000-acre sugar plantation, Madewood was the economic engine of Bayou Lafourche in the years before the Civil War. Doorways to the house's 23 rooms were framed with exotic

A giant moss-draped oak shades the cemetery that houses the remains of Madewood Plantation's first owner and his family. The ghost of a gateman has been detected near the entrance.

woods carved with custom designs. Each one is signed by the craftsman, Cornelius Hennessey. As with other plantations, Madewood disintegrated after the Civil War and suffered a severe economic depression throughout the latter half of the 19th century. In 1964, it was purchased by the Harold Marshall family and underwent a major restoration. Today, the plantation is beautifully furnished and open for tours and overnight guests.

The graveyard still has a creepy ambience left over from the Civil War years. The gate at the corner of the graveyard moves with creaking hinges, as if warning visitors that spirits lurk there. In fact, a male presence has been detected standing at the gate. Even on a warm day, he creates a cold spot and moves across your path as you pass through the gate. Psychic investigation suggests he is not a member of the Pugh family, but a slave whose job was to maintain the grounds, keeping the place free of weeds and greasing the iron hinges. This ghost has not been seen, but his presence is strong. He is not menacing and does not try to stop visitors from entering the graveyard. His purpose seems to be to inform visitors that the graves are being looked after and those who wander about the place should show proper respect for the dead of Madewood Plantation.

LA PETITE FILLE (THE LITTLE GIRL)

Houmas House Plantation
40136 Louisiana 942
Darrow 70725-2302
504-891-9494
www.houmashouse.com

The little girl caught the workmen by surprise. They might have been a little on edge, cautiously tearing up floors that were 150 years old, knowing that great people once walked the boards. But the men didn't expect to see the ghost of a little girl in the construction area. They watched as she descended the spiral staircase, puzzled by her presence and concerned for her safety. Before they could call out to her, she was gone. Over the next several days, the little girl—estimated to be between seven and ten years old—made many appearances. She was probably curious to see what the men were doing to her home, the great "Sugar Palace" known as Houmas House.

This ghost appeared so lifelike that witnesses described her in detail. She wore a blue dress and had dark eyes and brown hair. Apparently, she likes the renovations and restoration of the grand house, because she makes frequent appearances, usually in the morning or late in the afternoon. *La petite fille* has been seen tagging along after tour groups, skipping in the upstairs hallway, or descending the staircase where she was first spotted in 2003 by astonished workmen.

The identity of *la petite fille* has been narrowed down to two girls. Colonel John Preston and his wife, Caroline, assumed ownership of the grand plantation in 1825. Caroline's father, General Wade Hampton, built the manor house and established the plantation, which would eventually grow to 300,000 acres. Caroline and John

Houmas House Plantation is the jewel of the lower Mississippi and the home of a little ghost girl.

lost a daughter—probably to yellow fever—in 1848. They were so devastated by this tragedy that they left the plantation, never to return. It may be the ghost of this little girl that wanders the halls of Houmas House looking for her parents.

The second possibility is that she is the ghost of the daughter of a subsequent owner, Colonel William P. Miles and his wife, Harriet. They lost a seven-year-old daughter in 1900. She was buried in the estate's cemetery close to the Mississippi River. In 1927, the levee broke, washing away the headstones and covering the ground with tons of river silt. A new levee completed the destruction and desecration of the cemetery. This kind of disturbance often awakens spirits, causing them to wander about familiar places seeking help in restoring a grave that was to be a place of eternal rest.

Today, Houmas House Plantation has been restored to its former grandeur, and it is once again the crown jewel of Louisiana's River Road. Tours of the mansion and its surrounding grounds put visitors in touch with the antebellum era, when sugar was king and Houmas House was the richest of the rich. An alley of 200-year-old oak trees conveys visitors to the grand house, flanked on either side by garconnieres—living quarters for the plantation owner's adolescent sons—and surrounded by gardens and fountains. Ghost hunters may tour the home with docents then independently roam the grounds. The original French provincial house, constructed in the mid-1700s by original owners, Maurice Conway and Alexander Latil, stands behind the manor house. At times the building is crowded with visitors, but ghost hunters may detect cold spots and unexplained cold breezes and find orbs in their photographs.

THE GHOST COACHMAN

Nottoway Plantation
30970 Louisiana Highway 405
Whitecastle 70788
1-866-LA-SOUTH
www.nottoway.com

It is odd that Nottoway Plantation is not often included in books

During the Civil War, a Union gunboat fired on Nottoway Plantation until the commander remembered a previous visit to the house and ceased fire.

about haunted places in Louisiana. Folklorist and local writer Lyle Saxon claims that all of the old manor houses have a ghost or two. But Nottoway staff members who conduct tours don't talk about ghosts, and when pressed, they tend to deny that spirits walk the halls of the huge mansion. But I encountered a friendly spirit whose job was to welcome travelers and help them from their coaches and carriages.

With 53,000 square feet of living space, Nottoway is the largest plantation house in America. It was completed in 1859 for John Hampden Randolph, his wife, and their 11 children. With 155 field slaves and a large number of house slaves, the Randolphs were among the wealthiest of sugarcane planters in the years before the Civil War. Fearing the ravages of war and knowing the cotton market would be more lucrative than ever, Randolph left his plantation in the hands of his wife, took his four oldest children and several slaves, and established a cotton plantation in Texas. During the war, a Union gunboat, patrolling the Mississippi, fired on the great house. Mrs. Randolph stood of the front porch waving and shouting at the soldiers that she had several children in the house. By a stroke of luck, the gunboat commander ceased fire when he recalled he had been a guest in the house a year before the war. The house was saved from destruction by the social graces the Randolphs had extended to a Yankee. The lead balls fired at the house were dug out of the columns and put on display in the parlor.

The grand front porch of the huge house is accessed by two staircases. Between them, at ground level in the façade is a niche that accommodates one man. This was the duty station of a coachman, a slave whose job was to open the doors of carriages and assist passengers as they stepped down. He would also direct other slaves in unloading baggage and servicing the carriage or coach. The name of Nottoway's coachman is not known, but he is still on duty. A male presence can be detected in the niche, and sensitive ghost hunters feel a temperature drop when he is there. If you stand at the edge of the niche facing outward, you may feel the man standing behind you. He has been detected stepping out of the niche to the stone steps a few feet away as if he is preparing to unload a carriage that has just arrived.

GHOST OF THE FAITHFUL SERVANT

Cottage Plantation Ruins
River Road at Duncan Point,
six miles south of Magnolia Mound Plantation
Baton Rouge

Visitors driving River Road may get the impression that there are many historic plantation houses open for visitors or maintained as private homes. The fact is that few antebellum homes remain standing. Many were destroyed during the Civil War, while others fell into disrepair and failed financially during the later half of the 19th century. Without slave labor and eager markets for their cotton and sugar, these huge farms could not turn a profit or keep a staff to maintain the aging manor houses. Some of the old plantations survived into the 20th century before meeting with disaster. Cottage Plantation is one of them.

People looking for ghosts at the ruins of this plantation may be confused and led astray by Dennis William Hauck's brief report in his book *Haunted Places: The National Directory: Ghostly Abodes, Sacred Sites, UFO Landings and Other Supernatural Locations.* Hauck tells us the place is located about 40 miles north of Baton Rouge in St. Francisville. He gives the address of the Cottage Plantation, a bed-and-breakfast inn that occupies an old manor house, surrounded by several outbuildings. This is not the haunted ruins of the old riverfront Cottage Plantation.

The haunted ruins are located about six miles south of Baton Rouge on River Road. They sit about 75 yards from the road, surrounded by grazing cattle and a few of the yucca trees that once lined the driveway leading to the main house. There is no sign indicating the location of the ruins. Ghost hunters have to drive slowly, keeping a sharp eye on the traffic while scanning the fields to the left as they drive south. The area comprises Duncan's Point, a promontory that juts out into the Mississippi. In the 1820s, it was called Moore's Point. The first owner of the tract of land built a small summer cottage there. Subsequent owners paid tribute to the charming little house among the magnolias and wisterias by calling their stately mansion the "cottage."

In 1825, Abner Duncan bought a large tract of land at Moore's

Point from Armand Duplantier. He combined it with the neighboring Laiche tract and built a huge manor house he called Cottage Plantation. Later that year, he gave the estate to his daughter, Frances, and her husband, Frederick Conrad, as a wedding gift. They made the Cottage one of the most successful sugar plantations in the region.

Soon after the Conrads set up housekeeping in their wonderful new plantation, a strange man appeared on the porch asking for a drink, meal, and place to sleep. Angus Holt must have impressed the Conrads with his wit, charm, and intelligence, because he was invited to stay on as personal secretary to Conrad. As it turned out, Holt was a classical scholar and skilled in landscape design.

During the Civil War, the plantation was shelled by Union riverboats under the command of Conrad's nephew. The young officer later admitted he fired on his uncle's property merely to "annoy the old rebel." In spite of family relations, Conrad and Holt were imprisoned

The sad ruins of Cottage Plantation stand amid tall grass and sprawling trees. From a distance, visitors have spotted strange lights and the ghost of houseman Angus Holt.

during the war. Conrad died before the South surrendered. After the war, Holt returned to Cottage Plantation only to find most of the Conrad family dead or scattered. Always loyal to the family that gave him a home and warm companionship, he stayed on until 1880, serving as manager of the plantation. Even after his death, it seems Holt continued to care for the old plantation.

For decades, the ghost of Angus Holt was seen walking the galleries and hallways of the manor house. While alive, he had the habit of collecting bits of cloth, string, yarn, even dried biscuits. As a ghost, the habit continued. His pale figure was often seen holding scraps of cloth in his hand.

In 1960, Cottage Plantation was struck by lightning and burned to the ground. Many of its massive columns remain standing on the brick foundation. Today, these columns can be seen from River Road. People who stop to view them often see a tall, slim man with white hair roaming about the ruins. This pale figure, believed to be the ghost of Angus Holt, moves slowly, stepping through the grass and over crumbling piles of bricks, often carrying a scrap of cloth in his hand. Within moments of being spotted, the ghostly figure vanishes. Ghost hunters believe the ghost of Holt remains because of his great devotion to the Conrad family and love of the great house that was his home for more than 50 years.

There are other ghosts at Cottage Plantation. In 1859, the steamboat *Princess,* en route to New Orleans, exploded off Duncan's Point. Seventy people were killed instantly while more than a hundred made it to the shore at Cottage Plantation. White sheets were rolled out on the front lawn and covered with flour. Burn victims were placed on the sheets and rolled by slaves, covering their wounds with the flour. In spite of the attention of the entire plantation and the doctors who rushed to the scene from Baton Rouge, more than a hundred people died on the manor house lawn. Nearly 150 years later, ghostly clouds of white powder rise into the night air and pieces of the bloodied sheets are raised by the breezes off the river.

During the Civil War, the house was used as a hospital for Union soldiers. Many died there, filling a small cemetery that is now overgrown with grass. Ghostly figures in blue uniforms have been seen near the road in the evening. Most of them are missing a limb or two.

GHOST OF SENATOR PIERRE COUVILLON

Old State Capitol
Center for Political and Governmental History
100 North Boulevard (at River Road)
Baton Rouge 70801
225-342-0500
www.sec.state.la.us/museums/osc/osc/osc-index.htm

In 1832, Pierre Couvillon was elected to the Louisiana House of Representatives. He used his large physical presence—described as "gargantuan"—to intimidate political rivals while charming his constituents and anyone else who might support his causes. After successful terms in the House, Pierre was elected to the state senate, where his power, and the zeal of his opponents, increased. Foremost on his political agenda was the revision of the state's banking laws and regulations. In the 1840s, Louisiana's banking practices were best characterized as corrupt. They favored a small group of wealthy families who maintained their lucrative privileges by buying political support. Couvillon opposed them by lobbying his colleagues in both houses of the state legislature and exposing corrupt banking officials. By 1850, he had earned a reputation as an honest politician and champion of the welfare of the state's poor and middle class.

In 1852, while at home in Avoyelles Parish, Couvillon was preparing for the upcoming legislative session when he received word that a floodgate of financial payoffs had opened and many of his colleagues in the senate had lined up for large shares. Legend says that he was outraged and went on a rampage, shouting from the second-floor windows of his house and screaming at the top of his lungs. Apparently, he carried on for a long time, raising his blood pressure and heart rate to dangerously high levels. The rampage ended when Couvillon was struck down by a heart attack. He was buried in Mansura Catholic Cemetery, leaving his widow to care for their ten children. Louisiana lost one of its first reform legislators.

Pierre Couvillon believed so strongly in his crusade to clean up state banking practices and end political corruption in Louisiana that he refused to let death stand in his way. After his funeral, he traveled from his new home—Mansura cemetery—to the state capitol and resumed his work. Legend says that Couvillon's large presence was noted by fellow legislators until the onset of the Civil War. Couvillon's positions on the issues that led to the Civil War are not known, but many believe he stood with the state legislators in February 1861 when they voted to secede from the Union.

When the Union army swept through Baton Rouge in 1862, they burned the capitol building. For 20 years, its soot-stained walls stood, enclosing a pile of rubble. The state legislature was faced with the question of tearing down the tragic structure or rebuilding it. When the vote was taken, the ghostly hand of Pierre Couvillon was likely counted, assuring restoration of the grand building that was the site of his brilliant political career.

Today the state capitol stands on a hill looking more like an English castle than a government building. Inside, ornate woodwork and a spectacular cast-iron, brass-trimmed, spiral staircase amazes visitors, but the huge stained-glass dome that sits over the multistory lobby is breathtaking. The state legislature no longer meets in the building, but Senator Pierre Couvillon is there, keeping an eye on staff and visitors and sometimes expressing his approval or disapproval of the restoration.

In 1994, after another round of improvements, the Old State Capitol opened as the Louisiana Center for Political and Governmental History. Hauntings and ghostly activities often increase after remodeling or other major changes in a building. When the new center opened, Couvillon's ghost became quite active. At night, he triggered motion sensors, making the lone security guard extremely nervous. Sequential activation of these sensors indicated a disembodied being walked from a display of bedroom furniture from the governor's mansion housed in a room on the first floor to the adjacent room containing a dining-room display. The unseen visitor then walked up the grand spiral staircase to the second floor, down the hallway, finally stopping in the old senate chamber. At the time of this event, the only items in this huge room were a wooden desk enclosed by a wooden guardrail and a portrait of Senator Pierre Couvillon.

This ghost has left footprints on dusty floors of locked rooms, stolen tools and other objects from staff members working on displays, and creates cold spots. One maintenance supervisor reports that the capitol

The ghost of state senator Pierre Couvillon, who died in 1852, still shows up for votes in the Old State Capitol. The building was nearly destroyed by the Union army in 1862.

ghost has an affinity for pliers. Fifteen pairs of pliers have disappeared when they were left unused for a few seconds. The playful ghost also has lined up items such as screws that were left scattered on a desk.

Ghost hunters might experience the ghostly activity of Pierre Couvillon if they can spend a lot of time in the building's second-floor rooms. Crowds of visitors tend to ebb and flow, creating times when only the ghost hunter is present in the old senate chamber or smaller rooms on the floor. Leave a stack of coins on the floor, windowsill, or a desk for a few minutes. You may find them rearranged by the fastidious Pierre Couvillon.

GHOST CREW OF THE FIGHTING SHIP

USS *Kidd*
305 South River Road
Baton Rouge 70802-6220
225-342-1942
www.usskidd.com

Visitors walking the passageways of this World War II destroyer and looking about the crew's quarters and other below-deck compartments between the twin smokestacks might see sailors dressed in 1940s-era uniforms. These fellows are not docents in period costumes. They are the ghost crew of a fighting ship, the USS *Kidd.*

It has been said that all ships are haunted. These hauntings are believed to be the result of sailing in harm's way, desperate battles in which lives were lost, close calls in rough seas, and crew who experienced life-threatening illnesses or catastrophic injuries, including the loss of limbs through accident or combat. Also, crew members often spent long months at sea, with little hope of seeing their homes soon. They might have experienced emotions that created environmental imprints that, years later, are experienced by sensitive visitors. A love for the ship can also create emotional imprints. Some sailors who died ashore have been known to make ghostly appearances on the decks of the ships that were once their homes. Good examples are the aircraft carrier USS *Hornet,* berthed at Alameda, California, and the *Star of India* featured in San Diego's historic floating maritime museum.

All the elements mentioned above can be found in the history of the USS *Kidd* (DD 661). This *Fletcher*-class destroyer, known as the "Pirate of the Pacific," served in the Pacific during World War II and the Korean War. Named for Isaac C. Kidd, who died in the Pearl Harbor attack, the *Kidd*, with a complement of 34 officers and 295 enlisted crew, earned 12 battle stars for engagements with enemy submarines, surface ships, and aircraft. On April 11, 1945, during the battle for Okinawa, the *Kidd* was hit by a Japanese kamikaze. The suicidal pilot penetrated the ship's antiaircraft fire and slammed into the *Kidd*, killing 38 crewmen.

Many of these World War II heroes are still onboard. In the enlisted crew quarters and compartments on the starboard (right) side of the ship, partial apparitions of sailors have been seen by many visitors. Some surprised visitors have felt unexplained cold spots or icy breezes. Sensitive ghost hunters may detect the presence of the ghostly crew by a touch on the shoulder, a feeling that someone is hovering nearby, or a partial apparition. At locations such as the USS *Kidd*, where a disaster caused dismemberment, it is common to see the image of a solitary body part, such as a leg or an arm, moving as though it was still attached.

The USS *Kidd* is open to the public as a floating memorial to the destroyer crews of World War II. It is a popular attraction along Baton Rouge's riverfront but it is possible for ghost hunters to explore portions of the ship away from curious tourists. Overnight visits can be arranged.

THE SUICIDE BRIDE

Parlange Plantation House
8211 False River Road (Louisiana 1) at Highway 78 (Parlange Lane)
New Roads 70760-4001
225-638-8410
Private residence. Tours by appointment for a fee.

From the very beginning, Julie de Ternant had no choice in the matter. Her father, Claude de Ternant, son of the Marquis de Ternant, raised his family by the old, strict, French traditions by which he was raised. And by these traditions, it was his right and, as he saw it, his duty to select a husband for his charming daughter Julie. She was the youngest of his five children, and he assured her, he would do what was best for her. He had no doubt Julie would abide by his decision.

But the man whom Claude de Ternant selected for Julie was not someone she could love. In fact, as the story goes, she was repulsed by him. He was much older than her, and he was a heavy man who sweated profusely in Louisiana's humid air. But the year was 1790, and proper young ladies always obeyed their fathers, especially when the social position and wealth of the family would be enhanced by the union.

The wedding took place late in the day. The beautiful plantation home in which Julie had lived all her life was decked out with colorful flowers and garlands, and the yard was full of fancy guests. Looking at her new husband, Julie knew she could never love him. Some storytellers say she ran from the ceremony, never saying, "I do." Local legend says she held back her tears, honored her father's wishes, and went through with the unhappy ceremony. It was later that night that she faced the true horror of her predicament. As her new husband took her hand to lead her to bed, she bolted from the room. Screaming, she ran through the house, onto the gallery, and down the front stairs. Frantic to get away, she heard the heavy steps of her husband chasing after her.

It was a dark night, but having played on the steps many times, she raced down them, distancing herself from the panting, sweating man who stumbled behind her. The road was less than a hundred yards ahead, and beyond that, the false arm of the Mississippi River lay still and dark under a moonless sky. Her objective, if she had one in mind, will never be known. Julie might have planned on running down the road to a neighbor or throwing herself into the river. But, while dashing through darkness in the front yard of her father's plantation, she slammed into one of the oak trees that lined the front drive and died instantly. The next day, instead of starting a new life with a husband, Julie was buried in her wedding gown.

The painful, frightening final moments of her life left a strong imprint on the grounds of Parlange Plantation. Ghost hunters and surprised passersby have witnessed a young lady, dressed in a white gown, race down the steps of the house and run into a tree. At the instant of impact, the pale image vanishes. This ghost is seen after sunset, most often on nights when there is little or no moonlight.

Parlange Plantation is a private residence, but the oak-lined driveway and the ghost bride can be seen from outside the grounds. The 1750 French colonial house, built by the Marquis de Ternant on a 10,000-acre land grant, is a beautiful example of the upriver architectural style. The house and the ghost bride are well worth the side trip for travelers passing between Baton Rouge and St. Francisville on the west bank of the Mississippi River.

GHOST OF YOUNG WILLIAM TURNBULL

Rosedown Plantation
12501 Louisiana 10
St. Francisville 70775
225-635-3332
e-mail: rosedown@crt.state.la.us

William Turnbull grew up in a paradise named for an 1830s London play. Rosedown Plantation was a creation of his parents, Daniel and Martha Turnbull, who started construction of the manor house in 1834. When completed, Rosedown sprawled over 3,455 acres worked by 50 slaves. In addition to the two-story, French colonial-style house, buildings included a doctor's office, various barns, a house for the governess (Miss Nina's wing) and head housekeeper, and a gardener's cottage. Visitors approached the magnificent estate by a long driveway, lined with oak trees that passed through 28 acres of formal gardens. Today, Rosedown is a state historic site. It remains an impressive 371 acres—including Martha Turnbull's gardens—with 13 historic buildings.

Growing up on this huge estate must have been fun. William Turnbull and his brothers and sisters played in the formal gardens, fished in the lake behind the house, and enjoyed luxuries that were available to few in the United States. Just before the Civil War, Daniel Turnbull's cotton empire had made him one of the richest men in the country. But his power and money could not keep tragedy from his door.

In 1856, at the age of 27, William Turnbull had established his own plantation on DeSoto Island. It was nothing like his father's estate, but it was a very good start in the cotton business and destined to make William independently wealthy. Still, his heart remained at Rosedown, and he visited his family and childhood home often. Traveling by skiff across the river, often alone, he made the journey many times without mishap. But one day, the riverboat *Bella Donna*, steaming at high speed on water roughened by gusty winds, crossed his course and upset his craft. The steamboat's wake and choppy water were too much for the young man's swimming skills, and he drowned.

Daniel and Martha were devastated by the loss of their oldest son. It was a tragedy that lived with them until their deaths in 1861 and 1896, respectively. As an expression of their constant mourning, the ceiling of the south wing of the manor house is painted in black stripes. William's love for Rosedown Plantation, together with the longing of Daniel and Martha for their beloved eldest son, may be the reason why the young man remains at this St. Francisville plantation.

Curator Polly Luttrul and docents have had many experiences with the ghost of William Turnbull. He is a fun-loving ghost who enjoys playing with the electrical system of the house. After closing up at night, employees have had to go back into the house and turn off all the lights because William has turned them on. He likes the place brightly lit. Also, furniture has been inexplicably moved with traces of dried mud left on the floor, suggesting someone has come in from the gardens and pushed the heavy pieces out of place.

In the gardens, visitors have caught glimpses of a partial apparition dashing around the hedges or passing by the Greek statues placed there by Martha Turnbull. While walking through the gardens, I experienced the disembodied touch of someone on my left forearm. The sensation was that of a soft hand sweeping upward from my wrist to my elbow several times, raising the hair on my arm and slipping over my skin, moistened from the humid spring air.

The best evidence of a haunting at Rosedown Plantation was caught on film by a couple from Texas. Misty images of William's arm and neck were discovered in their photographs. He appeared to be placing his arm around the woman as she posed on the porch of the main house. At that moment, the woman felt an icy presence pass through her body.

In the back of the house by the lake, several cold spots have been

The ghost of William Turnbull roams the gardens and halls of Rosedown Plantation, enjoying his magnificent boyhood home.

found. Also, there are reports of cold spots, odd sensations, and the eerie presence of invisible beings in the kitchen—detached from the main house—and the old barn located near the parking lot. The spirit that haunts the barn is not pleased to have visitors and causes some ghost hunters to experience thick atmospheres and pushing sensations.

THE MOST HAUNTED HOUSE IN AMERICA

Myrtles Plantation
7747 U.S. 61
St. Francisville 70775
225-635-6277
www.myrtlesplantation.com

This stately, beautiful, aging mansion has been called one of "America's Most Haunted Homes." The big signs on U.S. 61, a few hundred feet from the entrance to the grand estate, declare it so. Several authors and producers of television programs have also proclaimed the Myrtles a genuine haunted house. Even the Smithsonian Institution recognizes that paranormal phenomena occur here. In the spring of 2005, the Atlantic Paranormal Society (TAPS) conducted a surveillance of the property and found evidence of ghostly activity. The staff of this historic and popular bed-and-breakfast inn, as well as hundreds of visitors, have had enough spooky experiences to convince the most hardened skeptic that many spirits of the dead reside at the amazing Myrtles Plantation in St. Francisville.

A ghost hunter's first paranormal experience may occur at the turn from busy U.S. 61 through the tall white gates of the Myrtles. Two ghosts have been spotted there. A gateman, whose job was to greet arriving guests and direct them to the parking area, quit after he watched a woman dressed in a long white dress pass through the gate. The gateman saw her walk up the drive and disappear as she approached the front door of the house. Visitors sometimes see a former caretaker who was killed in 1927 during a foiled robbery at one of the outbuildings. This fellow discourages visitors by telling them the plantation is closed or the inn is no longer open for business. Some visitors with reservations drive up to the estate office and ask the staff if the gentleman at the gate is correct. With a knowing smile, staff members of this famous mansion assure them the Myrtles is open and that their fascinating experience has just begun. It may continue for guests who stay in the caretaker's cottage. A recent ghost hunt by TAPS recorded the movement of a lamp in the cottage. Others have seen the face of the ghostly caretaker looking out the windows of his former home.

In 1797, General David Bradford purchased 600 acres of land that included an ancient Tunica Indian burial ground. On a prominent mound, he built an eight-room house and named the place Laurel Grove. Within days of moving into the house, Bradford became the first to spot a ghost there. In his diary, he mentioned the pale image of a naked Indian girl wandering the grounds. From that time forward, Bradford's plantation was known as a haunted place.

The tumultuous history of the plantation includes stories that proclaim the presence of at least ten ghosts. Some of these stories have come under close scrutiny by skeptics, traditional historians, paranormal debunkers, and ghost hunters trying to separate fact from fiction and fantasy. Most ghost hunters agree that this place is haunted by several ghosts, including the famous slave girl Chloe and murder victim William Winter.

After a few years of living at the plantation alone, Bradford moved his wife and five children from their home in Pennsylvania. At that time, the house consisted of four large rooms on each of two floors. After his death in 1817, Bradford's eldest daughter, Sarah Mathilda, married a lawyer, Clark Woodrooff. Woodrooff took over management of the plantation, and eventually, he and his wife became its owners. Local legend that has spread far and wide says that their house slave Chloe was responsible for three murders that ultimately gave rise to four ghosts.

Chloe was a young slave girl who worked inside the manor house. Her work was hard, and the days were long, but it was far better than working in the fields. House work afforded more opportunities to observe interesting, educated people, wear better clothing, and eat better food. The affairs of the busy Woodrooff family fascinated her and aroused her curiosity, and she did not go unnoticed by Judge Woodrooff. Following the custom of the day, the judge took Chloe as his mistress, having many sexual encounters with her.

The traditional story says that Chloe's curiosity got the best of her one afternoon, when she eavesdropped on the judge's private conversation with a visitor. Enraged, the judge ordered that Chloe's ear be cut off as a constant reminder of her failure to abide by household rules. She covered her disfigurement with a turban. To make matters worse, Chloe was sent to work in the fields.

Soon, the clever Chloe devised a plan to regain the trust of the Woodrooffs and her position in the house. On the occasion of the eldest daughter's ninth birthday, Chloe baked a cake and added the poisonous juice of oleander leaves. It is said that Chloe's objective was to make the children ill, then come to the rescue and nurse them back to health. Knowing the cause of the illness was to be Chloe's key to success in this terrible scheme.

Unfortunately, too much juice or the concentrating effects of baking made the cake lethal. By the end of the day, two of the Woodrooff children and their mother were desperately ill. The oleander juice had an effect similar to arsenic. Horrified by the tragic outcome, Chloe ran from the house to the slave quarters. She confessed her scheme, hoping someone might know a cure. But sometime in the night, Sarah Woodrooff and two of her children died. Fearing the judge might hold the entire slave quarters responsible, the slaves pulled Chloe from a shack and hanged her from a tall tree near the house. Later, they weighted her body with stones and threw her in the Mississippi, denying her a grave.

In that one terrible night, four people died at the Myrtles, creating four ghosts. Guests staying in the Ruffin Stirling room report seeing the children huddled at the fireplace, in the final hours of their agony. Convulsing with stomach pains, vomiting, crying, and too weak to stand, the ghosts of the Woodrooff children reenact the final moments of their lives. Guests in adjacent rooms have heard the crying and other sounds of children suffering through their poisoning. This kind of paranormal event is more likely an environmental imprint, or haunting, rather than ghosts repeating the act of dying.

The ghost of Sarah Woodrooff creates strong floral scents. The fragrances of roses, magnolias, and perfumes are often detected in the upstairs foyer and in some of the bedrooms. Sarah's apparition may be one of the images seen in the mirror that hangs in the downstairs foyer. Nearly everyone who views the famous haunted mirror sees unexplainable images that resemble hands, a head, and the outline of a woman in a long dress. Southern tradition called for all mirrors to be covered with black cloths whenever a death occurred in a house. If this was not done, the spirit of the deceased could enter the mirror and be trapped in the house. The night the Woodrooff children and their mother died, the household was in a state of shock and confusion, and the mirror in the foyer was not covered.

Photographs of the mirror often capture ghostly images, including the reflection of a woman descending the staircase. This may be the ghost of Mary Cobb Winter, who held her husband as he died on the 17th step. Myrtles tour guide Hester Eby explains that the glass has been replaced several times over the years. But each time new glass is installed, the ghostly images reappear.

Many people believe the spirits of the Myrtles Plantation's murder victims are trapped in the mirror that hangs in the home's foyer.

The ghost of Chloe has been captured in at least two famous photographs now on display at the Myrtles. One shows the dead slave hanging by her neck from a tall tree. The other amazing photograph shows a small black woman standing between the main house and the adjacent kitchen. This photo has been subjected to several scientific investigations and concluded to be a genuine photograph of a small woman dressed in clothing of the 1820s. In the course of one of these investigations, the ghosts of two children were discovered perched on the roof overlooking the rear yard. These ghosts may be the Woodrooff children or other children who died of yellow fever at the Myrtles. Visitors have seen lifelike children playing on the galleries, walking near the pond, and peeking in the window of the game room moments before they vanished.

Ghost hunters have searched the grounds for Chloe, and some believe they have located the tree from which she was hanged. The slave girl has been seen in the main house, too. Guests sometimes feel themselves tucked into bed by unseen hands. Some have awakened to see a black woman wearing a turban standing at the bedside. Female visitors who tour the house are warned that Chloe might snatch an earring or hair pin. Several women and girls have finished their tour only to find these items missing. In every case, only one earring is taken to satisfy the needs of a woman with only one ear.

This history of a horrible night of poisoning and a hanging may consist of facts and elements that have been embellished over the years as the story is repeated to new generations of fascinated listeners. Historians have uncovered inconsistencies that contradict the popular story presented in several books and portrayed in television programs. But many agree the spirits of the Woodrooff children and their mother haunt the Myrtles Plantation.

In 1834, Laurel Grove was purchased by the wealthy Ruffin Grey Stirling family. The Stirlings doubled the size of the house, adding a large foyer, twin parlors (one for ladies and one for gentlemen), a day sleeping room, and a downstairs bedroom. They widened and extended the galleries, and several rooms were included in the second-floor addition. They brought artisans from Europe to add magnificent plaster moldings and medallions and to install crystal chandeliers, Carrara marble mantles, and the cast-iron work along the galleries. Even then, the place had a reputation for being haunt-ed. Taking no chances, Mary Catherine Stirling added many features to ward off evil spirits. She had replicas of acanthus leaves carved into the plaster moldings and cherubs added to the chandeliers. Also, she had the locks turned upside down and the keyholes covered to con-fuse spirits' attempts to gain entry to the house and the windows at the front and rear of the grand foyer painted with crosses and plaster miniatures of the heads of nuns. Since the plantation's reputation for ghostly activity was tied to its name—Laurel Grove—the Stirlings changed the name to the Myrtles, no doubt inspired by the crepe myrtles that surround the house.

Despite their wealth and high position in Louisiana society, the Stirlings were not strangers to tragedy. Only four years after complet-ing major renovations to the house, Ruffin Grey Stirling died on July 17, 1854, leaving his wife to look after their vast holdings and nine children. Mary Catherine Stirling took up the reins and gained a rep-utation as a remarkable woman, an able manager of her four planta-tions, and a skilled business person. But her bad luck continued. Only four of her nine children lived long enough to marry. The eld-est son, Louis, was shot in the game room by a visitor who demand-ed payment of a gambling debt. Yellow fever and other illnesses took their toll on the family as well.

The Civil War virtually destroyed most plantations, including the Myrtles. Union soldiers looted the plantation and took most of the family's keepsakes and other personal mementoes. During the war, a tutor was shot in the gentlemen's parlor, and a Confederate soldier, a local boy known to the family, sought refuge at the Myrtles only to die in the upstairs bedroom now called the John Leake room. Financial disaster continued after the war, and the Stirlings lost own-ership of the Myrtles from April 1868 to April 1870. Shortly after regaining the deed, Mary's son-in-law was murdered on the side gallery.

It is believed that many of the Stirling tragedies have resulted in ghosts who still reside at the Myrtles. Visitors have detected the strong odor of cigar smoke in the John Leake room as the ghost of the Confederate soldier savors the final pleasure he knew before dying. His uniform is sometimes seen hanging in the armoire. Guests

who stay in the Ruffin Stirling room report the sound of children crying. While some people believe this haunting is created by the
Woodrooff children who died from the slave's poison, it is more likely a residual impression from the Stirling children, some of whom
died of yellow fever in the 1850s.

Kate Stirling Winter, granddaughter of Mary Stirling, died from
yellow fever at the age of three in 1861. Willing to try anything to
save her, the family called a voodoo priestess to the house. All of her
spells and incantations failed, though, leaving Kate and the priestess
to haunt the Myrtles. Kate's sadness and agony can be detected in the
upstairs room in which she died, now known as the General David
Bradford suite. The ghost of the voodoo priestess is seen wearing a
green head scarf resembling a turban and a long dress. This ghost has
appeared lifelike to many overnight visitors and holds a candle that
illuminates the room. It is suspected that this ghost is the entity who
often appears at the bedside and creates the frequent experience of
being tucked into bed. Some ghost investigators believe the ghostly
image seen in the famous Myrtles photograph is not that of Chloe,
but of the voodoo priestess.

The best documented murder at the Myrtles was that of William
Winter. On June 3, 1852, Winter married Sara Mulford Stirling,
daughter of the Myrtles owners, Ruffin Grey Stirling and his wife,
Mary. Twelve years after Stirling's death on July 17, 1864, Winter
became the business manager for Mary Stirling's vast holdings. He
managed to keep her four plantations and other assets together until
1867, when the estate faced bankruptcy. In December 1867, the
Myrtles was sold, but the family regained ownership in 1870 when
Sara Winter purchased it, probably through the skillful financial
maneuvers of her husband, William Winter. This unlikely process
suggests that William had a good mind for handling money, putting
together complex deals, and manipulating his partners, opponents,
and rivals. His business dealings may have led to his early demise.

In the evening of January 26, 1871, a rider approached the house
and called out for Mr. Winter, who was teaching a Sunday-school lesson in the gentlemen's parlor. As William stepped out on the side
gallery, the rider pulled a gun and shot him in the chest. The official
account states that William died on the spot, but the ghost story says

The Myrtles Plantation is considered one of the most haunted homes in America. With the ghosts of numerous murder victims and several others, including slaves and Civil War soldiers, the home is a must-see for ghost hunters.

that he staggered through the twin parlors, across the foyer, and climbed the steps, calling out for Sara, who was upstairs. William made it to the 17th step, where he met Sara and died in her arms. Staff of the inn, and many visitors, have heard William's heavy footsteps as he climbs the 17 steps to his death. The disembodied footfalls always rise, never descend. Sometimes a woman's voice is also heard crying out for William.

Devastated by her husband's murder, Sara Winter spent her remaining years as a recluse. She never left the Myrtles and spent most of her time in her room—now called the Judge Clark Woodruff suite—in a rocking chair. The chair has since been removed from the room but guests report hearing its repetitive creaking as it rocks on the floor. An intense floral fragrance has also been detected in the room and elsewhere in the house, reminiscent of the strong perfumes of the 1870s.

GHOST OF THE REBEL SPY

Loyd Hall
292 Loyd Bridge Road
Cheneyville 71325-9142
318-776-5641

In death, as in life, the ghost of William Loyd is playful, inquisitive, and a bit of a trouble maker. As a young man in England—a member, not in good standing, of the Lloyd's of London insurance dynasty—his exploits so embarrassed the family that they banished him to America, never to return to England. As he stepped aboard the ship, they endowed him with a small fortune with which to start anew. In return, the family demanded that William drop one of the *l*s from his name, further separating him from the rest of the proud family.

In 1820, William Loyd purchased a large tract of land and built Loyd Hall Plantation. With 60 slaves, he established a plantation that profited from tobacco, cotton, indigo, and sugarcane. Unable to resist meddling in the affairs of local Indians, he created unrest in the region that resulted in Choctaw attacks on his manor house. During the Civil War, Loyd spied for both the Confederate and Union armies. Relishing the role of double agent, he played one side against the other, perhaps seeking to protect Loyd Hall Plantation from destruction. Late in 1864, his duplicity backfired. Union forces pronounced him guilty of counterespionage and placed Loyd under house arrest. After a few days of complete isolation in an upstairs bedroom, he was dragged from his house, tarred and feathered, and hung from an oak tree within view of his family and slaves. During his 44 years in America, the blue-blood Brit was known by several nicknames including Wylie Willy and the Doggone Trickster.

After William's death, his brother, James, kept the plantation going until 1871. James sold the place for unspecified reasons and was followed by a string of 21 owners over a period of 71 years. Despite fertile soil and good markets for the plantation's crops, none turned a profit. One reason may be the horrible death of the plantation's founder and his restless ghost.

William's ghostly activity includes the kinds of tricks he was known for when he was alive. He opens the front door to the mansion, creates the sound of heavy footsteps, strokes the keys of the piano, and opens and closes cabinet doors. The ghost also moves silverware and other table service, particularly if important guests have gathered for dinner. In several rooms of the house, visitors have experienced William's warm breath on their necks and, sometimes, the touch of his hand. He also creates cold spots and unexplained icy breezes.

The ghost of Inez Loyd, William's niece, also haunts Loyd Hall. Her wedding was held in the mansion, complete with wagonloads of flowers, a grand banquet, an orchestra, and the region's finest folks dressed in their fanciest clothes. As Inez completed her walk down the aisle, she noticed her groom had not yet made his appearance. Slowing her pace, thinking he would arrive at any second, her anxiety and embarrassment grew to intolerable levels. Finding herself at the end of the aisle, she turned to face her guests, burst into tears, and ran to her room on the third floor. She waited until the guests had departed and there was no chance that her groom would show up, perhaps mangled by some accident or in the throes of a disabling illness, then jumped through a window and fell to her death.

The ghost of Anne Loyd sometimes calls out the names of house staff. She has been seen on the first floor near the kitchen and back hallway. Anne appears as a tall, slender woman in a black dress. She appears only briefly before vanishing into the walls. Visitors note an atmosphere of grief when this ghost is present.

Another female ghost, nanny Sally Boston, also roams the mansion. Sally, a black woman, has been seen in both white and black dresses, with a long, white apron. Her head is capped by a turban. The slave nanny is a kindly, benevolent ghost in spite of the poisoning that led to her death. She does have objections to candles being placed on the mantle in the back parlor, though. Witnesses have seen them knocked to the floor by an invisible hand.

Sally Boston is not the only ghost seen in the back parlor. The partial apparition of a Union soldier, Harry Henry, has surprised house staff and guests as well. Nothing more than polished black boots and the tip of a saber scabbard are seen there, but elsewhere in the house, the ghost of Harry Henry has appeared completely lifelike. During the Civil War, Union troops occupied the house and took over the entire plantation. In spite of the execution of William Loyd by Union officers, a young woman in the Loyd household fell in love with the Yankee Harry Henry. When the troops departed the plantation, Henry could not tear himself away from his Southern sweetheart. He deserted the army and hid in the attic. After a few days, when his food and water ran out, he ventured downstairs, under the cover of darkness, to join his young lady. Unfortunately, he ran into Grandma Loyd, who had not been informed that her son's niece was keeping a young man hidden in the attic. Startled, she pulled a pistol and shot the man thinking him a renegade Yankee. It is said that the would-be lover was buried in a shallow grave under the house. Henry's desire to become a member of the Loyd family has bound his spirit to the mansion.

When the Fitzgeralds purchased the plantation in 1948, they had no idea the ghost of Harry Henry would join their family. As little girls, Paige and Melinda Fitzgerald discovered a playmate on the third floor of their home. He appeared as a tall, dark man dressed in a blue uniform. Henry filled their hours, day after day, with games and stories. The girls played with him for years, not realizing that he was a ghost. As an adult, Melinda recalled to her mother that Henry was "like a big brother to us . . . He was the nicest person." Henry was also a talented violinist. Sweets notes from his instrument are heard late at night coming from the second-floor balcony. His heavy footsteps are often heard pacing the attic floor. He may be distressed by the sight of his blood that reportedly stained the floorboards.

Today, Loyd Hall Plantation is a popular bed-and-breakfast inn and venue for special events such as weddings. Tours of the manor house and grounds are conducted hourly. Ghostly activity at this historic plantation is best appreciated by staying a night or two in one of the guest cottages. Guests in the Commissary have reported hearing screams during the night. In Minda's House, spirits move the bed. In the McCullough House, ghosts turn the lights on while guests are asleep. Ghosts who haunt the plantation also like to manipulate stacks of coins or decks of cards left on a nightstand while guests are asleep or out of the room.

GHOST OF FELICITE AND THE MURDERED PIRATE

Chretien Point Plantation
665 Chretien Point Road
Sunset 70584
337-662-7050
www.chretienpoint.com

Felicite was alone but not helpless. Her husband, Hypolite Chretien, son of the plantation's builder, Joseph Chretien, had died in 1839. This tragedy came only one year after the couple lost their eldest son to yellow fever. Felicite dressed every day in traditional mourning black, but gathered her strength and assumed duties that were never performed by women. Instead of hiring an overseer for the 640-acre cotton plantation, she put on pants, mounted a horse, and kept the slaves in the fields. Relishing her newfound power and independence, Felicite began smoking cigars, playing poker, and even rekindled some of her husband's nefarious business dealings.

Joseph Chretien had close ties with the pirate Jean Lafitte. It is not clear why Lafitte traveled inland so far from the banks of the Mississippi to carry on his illegal business, but he often used Chretien Point grounds to stage sales of stolen goods, including undocumented slaves. It seems that Felicite allowed this practice to continue. By 1839, Lafitte himself may have moved on to Texas or died, but his followers continued to conduct business at Chretien Point with the approval of Felicite, or in spite of her objections.

It didn't take long for these fellows to see that Felicite was rich, alone in the big house at night, and vulnerable to attack. By the early 1840s, her wealth included 3,000 acres of farmlands and $250,000 in other assets. Added to that, Felicite wore her jewelry even when riding over her vast estate and when she conducted business. One night, she was awakened by the sound of horses approaching the house. Within minutes, the front door flew open, and the sound of heavy boots upon the floor echoed up the stairs. In an instant, Felicite knew what was happening. She stepped from her room and stood at the top of the stairs as a pirate started up from the foyer. With amazing confidence, she descended a few steps and held out a necklace as an offering coupled with a plea to take the prize and leave the house.

The pirate ascended the stairs, his eyes focused only on the dazzling jewels. As he placed his foot on the 11th step, Felicite raised a gun that had been hidden in her gown and shot the thief between the eyes. He fell on the 11th step and died in a puddle of his blood. On hearing the shot, his companions fled as Felicite's slaves ran from their quarters to the manor house.

Felicite's loyal slaves pulled the body from the stairs and stuffed it in a small closet beneath the staircase. The slaves spent the rest of the night scrubbing the stairs, trying to remove the blood stains. Later, the dead pirate was carted from the house and buried in an unmarked grave somewhere on the plantation. People who work in this house— now a popular inn—and guests can attest that the pirate is still there. His footsteps have been heard as his ghost climbs the staircase. His disembodied sounds are also heard in the dining room and parlor. Psychic investigation of the house revealed that the pirate's name is Robert, pronounced in the French style. Today, he is not menacing, just curious. There is some indication that he likes to manipulate coins. For a long period in 2003, pennies were found all over the second floor of the house. Ghost hunters who spend a night in the Chretien Point manor house may experience Robert's ghostly presence by leaving a stack of coins on a nightstand. In the morning, or after leaving the room for a while, the coins are often scattered or missing.

The ghosts of Felicite Chretien and her daughter-in-law, Celestine, also often appear in the house. Celestine's portrait hangs over the fireplace where it was placed in 1846. Her ghost, dressed in a white gown, appears in the dining room. She has spoken to house staff and offered comforting words at stressful times. Contractors working in the house have also seen Celestine. One man, after watching the apparition glide across the room in which he was working, picked up his tools and quit.

Felicite appears often in the Magnolia room on the second floor. Visitors walking the grounds, as well as staff members, have seen her ghost in the window holding back the lace curtains. Witnesses described details of her appearance, including a wide-brimmed hat with black netting that hung to her waist. This is the traditional mourning attire of Creole women that Felicite wore everyday.

Ghostly remnants of a Civil War battle—the Battle of Little Carrion Crow Bayou—are seen on the plantation. In this 1863 clash between Union and Confederate troops, the house was caught in the crossfire and riddled with bullets. The roof was nearly destroyed by cannon fire. The house was saved from total destruction by a Masonic distress signal, sent by Felicite's son, Hypolite II, to the Union commander who, fortunately, was also a Mason. After the battle, Felicite fed the starving Union soldiers while the Confederate dead were buried in a mass grave by her slaves. Apparitions of these rebel troops are often seen marching across the ground of Chretien Point plantation. Some of them pass through the house, appearing only from the waist down. A Confederate officer known as "the General" has also been seen in the plantation office and by the pond. He may be responsible for the odor of cigar smoke detected at various sites on the first floor.

Ghost hunters who visit this plantation should also visit nearby Marland Bridge. Union soldier William Marland earned the Congressional Medal of Honor by charging this bridge held by the 11th Texas Infantry. Many men died there, leaving spirit remnants and environmental imprints. The ghosts of a little girl, killed in 1922 when she was hit by a car, and a teenage girl murdered there in the 1970s, also wander this site. It has been reported that horses and dogs are afraid to cross Marland Bridge. Local riders must dismount and walk their horses through the site.

Once a month, Chretien Point Plantation hosts a ghost dinner that is an absolute must for ghost hunters. This event includes a delightful reception, tour of the great house with entertaining and knowledgeable guides, and a three-course meal in the plantation's formal dining room. (See Appendix D.) It is reported that 90 percent of guests at this plantation experience some kind of paranormal activity. This high rating places Chretien Point Plantation near the top of the list of America's most haunted houses.

APPENDIX A

Sighting Report Form

Photocopy and enlarge the form on the next page to a standard 8.5 x 11 inch format. This form should be completed right after a sighting. If the ghost hunt is performed by a group, a designated leader should assume the role of reporter. The reporter is responsible for completing this form.

The reporter and each witness should make a statement, either audio or written, describing in full their experiences at the site. Date, sign, and label these statements with a reference number identical to the report number on the sighting report form. Attach the statements to the report form.

SIGHTING REPORT

SITE NAME _____ REPORT # _____
LOCATION _____ DATE: _____
_____ TIME: _____
REPORTER _____ SITE # _____
WITNESSES _____

DESCRIPTION OF APPARITION

_____

temperature change   [] YES   [] NO
auditory phenomena   [] YES   [] NO
telekinesis   [] YES   [] NO
visual phenomena   [] YES   [] NO
other phenomena   [] YES   [] NO
Description: _____

Use the reverse side for diagrams, maps, and drawings.

SPECIFIC LOCATION WITHIN SITE: _____

PREVIOUS SIGHTINGS AT THIS SITE?
                      [] YES   [] NO
Reference: _____

Summary: _____

RECORDS:
audio   [] YES   [] NO   Ref. No. _____
video   [] YES   [] NO   Ref. No. _____
photo   [] YES   [] NO   Ref. No. _____
Summary of Records: _____

Disposition of Records: _____

WITNESS STATEMENTS (Summary): _____

audio   [] YES   [] NO
written   [] YES   [] NO
Disposition of statements: _____

APPENDIX B

Suggested Reading

BOOKS

Anderson, Jean. *The Haunting of America.* Boston: Houghton-Mifflin, 1973.

Arthur, Stanley Clisby. *Old New Orleans: Walking Tours of the French Quarter.* Gretna, LA: Pelican Publishing Co., 1995.

Auerbach, Loyd. *ESP, Hauntings, and Poltergeists.* New York: Warner Books, 1986.

——. *Ghost Hunting: How to Investigate the Paranormal.* Oakland, CA: Ronin Publishing, 2004.

Bardens, Dennis. *Ghosts and Hauntings.* Lincoln, NE: IUniverse, 2000.

Beckett, John. *World's Weirdest True Ghost Stories.* New York: Sterling Publishing, 1992.

Browne, Sylvia. *Adventures of a Psychic.* New York: Penguin Books, 1990.

Cohen, Daniel. *The Encyclopedia of Ghosts.* New York: Dodd, Mead Publishers, 1984.

Cornell, Tony. *Investigating the Paranormal.* New York: Helix Press, 2002.

DeBart, Jess. *Plantations of Louisiana.* Gretna, LA: Pelican Publishing Co., 2001.

Dickinson, Joy. *Haunted City: An Unauthorized Guide to the Magical, Magnificent New Orleans of Anne Rice.* New York: Citadel Press, 2004.

Dwyer, Jeff. *Ghost Hunter's Guide to Los Angeles.* Gretna, LA: Pelican Publishing Co., 2007.

——. *Ghost Hunter's Guide to the San Francisco Bay Area.* Gretna, LA: Pelican Publishing Co., 2005.

Ebon, Martin, ed. *The Signet Handbook of Parapsychology.* New York: New American Library, 1978.

Florence, Robert. *New Orleans Cemeteries: Life in the Cities of the Dead.* New Orleans: Batture Press, 1997.

Hauck, Dennis William. *Haunted Places: The National Directory.* New York: Penguin Group, 2002.

Holzer, Hans. *Ghosts I've Met.* New York: Barnes and Noble, 2005.

——. *Ghosts: True Encounters with the World Beyond.* New York: Black Dog and Leventhal Publishers, 2004.

——. *Hans Holzer's Travel Guide to Haunted Houses.* New York: Black Dog and Leventhal Publishers, 1999.

——. *Real Hauntings.* New York: Barnes and Noble, 1995.

——. *True Ghost Stories.* New York: Barnes and Noble, 2001.

Huber, Leonard V. *New Orleans: A Pictorial History.* Gretna, LA: Pelican Publishing Co., 1991.

Klein, Victor C. *New Orleans Ghosts.* Metairie, LA: Lycanthrope Press, 1993.

——. *New Orleans Ghosts, Volume 3.* Metairie, LA: Lycanthrope Press, 2005.

MacKenzie, Andrew. *Hauntings and Apparitions.* London: Granada Publishing, 1982.

Martinez, Raymond J. *Marie Laveau, Voodoo Queen.* Gretna, LA: Pelican Publishing Co., 2001.

Mead, Robin. *Haunted Hotels: A Guide to American and Canadian Inns and Their Ghosts.* Nashville: Rutledge Hill Press, 1995.

Montz, Larry, and Deanna Smoller. *ISPR Investigates: The Ghosts of New Orleans.* Atglen, PA: Whitefor Press, 2000.

Morgan, Heather. *Frommer's Irreverent Guide to New Orleans.* New York: Wiley Publishing, 2002.

Pascoe, Jill. *Louisiana's Plantation Homes.* Baton Rouge, LA: Irongate Press, 2004.

Ramsland, Katherine. *Ghost: Investigating the Other Side.* New York: St. Martin's Press, 2001.

Rogo, Scott. *Mind Beyond the Body.* New York: Penguin Books, 1978.

———. *The Poltergeist Experience.* New York: Penguin Books, 1979.

Rule, Leslie. *Coast to Coast Ghosts: True Stories of Hauntings Across America.* Kansas City, MO: Andrews McMeel Publishing, 2001.

Saxon, Lyle, Edward Dreyer, and Robert Tallant. *Gumbo Ya-Ya: Folk Tales of Louisiana.* Gretna, LA: Pelican Publishing Co., 1987.

Saxon, Lyle. *Fabulous New Orleans.* Gretna, LA: Pelican Publishing Co., 1988.

Sillery, Barbara. *The Haunting of Louisiana.* Gretna, LA: Pelican Publishing Co., 2003.

Smith, Kalila Katherine. *Journey Into Darkness: Ghosts and Vampires of New Orleans.* New Orleans: De Simonin Publications, 1998.

Southall, Robert. *How to be a Ghost Hunter.* St. Paul: Llewellyn Publications, 2003.

Spaeth, Frank. *Phantom Army of the Civil War and Other Southern Ghost Stories.* Edison, NJ: Castle Books, 2000.

Taylor, Troy. *Ghost Hunter's Guidebook.* Alton, IL: Whitechapel Productions Press, 1999.

———. *Haunted New Orleans.* Alton, IL: Whitechapel Productions Press, 2000.

Warren, Joshua P. *How to Hunt for Ghosts: A Practical Guide.* New York: Fireside Press, 2003.

Wlodarski, Robert, and Anne Wlodarski. *Southern Fried Spirits: A Guide to Haunted Restaurants, Inns and Taverns.* Plano, TX: Republic of Texas Press, 2000.

ARTICLES

Associated Press. "Ghost buster: Ohio woman inspires CBS' supernatural series." *Boston Herald,* July 4, 2005.

Barrett, Greg. "Can the living talk to the dead? Psychics say they connect with the other world, but skeptics respond: 'Prove it.'" *USA Today,* June 20, 2001.

Cadden, Mary. "Get spooked on a walking tour." *USA Today,* October 17, 2003.

Cannizaro, Steve. "Armory ghost lingers." *New Orleans Times-Picayune,* October 31, 1998.

Fox, Carol. "Ghostbuster to tell secrets of the hunt." *Los Angeles Times,* October 28, 1989.

Grose, Thomas. "Ghost scare up good business in Britain." *USA Today,* August 22, 1996.

Guillot. Craig. "Cemeteries get eerie in Big Easy, land of voodoo, ghosts and jazz." *Detroit Free Press,* October 17, 2004.

Hernandez, Daniel. "Little Shop of Santeria." *Los Angeles Times,* July 7, 2005.

Hill, Angela. "Paranormal experts say it's not all funny." *Oakland (CA) Tribune,* October 18, 2002.

Hunter, Mark H. "Laura Plantation home rises from the ashes." *Baton Rouge Advocate,* May 22, 2005.

LaFee, Scott. "Ghost busted: Home study course in spirit hunting is certifiable." *San Diego Union,* October 31, 2002.

"Lloyd Auerback shares tales from the dark side." *San Francisco Chronicle,* October 30, 1998.

Loar, Russell. "She's there when things go bump in the night." *Los Angeles Times,* May 26, 1997.

Massingill, T. "Business of ghost busting." *Contra Costa Times,* October 8, 2000.

Moran, Gwen. "Real-life ghost busters." *USA Weekend,* October 31, 2004.

Pilcher, Steve. "Wine and spirits." *San Francisco Chronicle,* October 28, 2004.

Schenden, Laurie. "Attractions: scaring up some business." *Los Angeles Times,* June 15, 2000.

"Spirits, specters and strange sightings abound at America's most haunted hotels." *Los Angeles Times,* October 15, 2003.

APPENDIX C

Films, DVDs, and Videos

Fictional films may provide information that will assist you in preparing yourself for a ghost hunt. This assistance ranges from putting you in the proper mood for ghost hunting to useful techniques for exploring haunted places and information about the nature of ghostly activity.

The Amityville Horror (1979). Directed by Stuart Rosenberg, starring James Brolin and Margot Kidder.

The Canterville Ghost (1996, made for TV). Directed by Sidney Macartney. Starring Patrick Stewart.

Carrie (1976). Directed by Brian De Palma. Starring Sissy Spacek and Piper Laurie.

Cemetery Man (1994). Directed by Michele Soavi. Starring Rupert Everett and Francois Hadji-Lazaro.

Changeling (1980). Directed by Peter Medak. Starring George C. Scott and Trish VanDevere.

City of Angels (1998). Directed by Brad Silberling. Starring Nicolas Cage and Meg Ryan.

Dragonfly (2002). Directed by Tom Shadyac. Starring Kevin Costner and Kathy Bates.

The Entity (1983). Directed by Sidney J. Furie. Starring Barbara Hershey and Ron Silver.

Frighteners (1996). Directed by Peter Jackson. Starring Michael J. Fox and Trini Alvarado.

Ghost (1990). Directed by Jerry Zucker. Starring Patrick Swayze and Demi Moore.

Ghost of Flight 409 (1987, made for TV). Directed by Steven Hilliard Stern. Starring Ernest Borgnine and Kim Basinger.

Ghost Ship (2002). Directed by Steve Beck. Starring Julianna Margulies and Ron Eldard.

Ghosts of California (2003). Documentary.

Ghosts of England and Belgrave Hall (2001). Documentary.

Ghost Stories, Volumes 1 and 2 (1997). Documentaries hosted by Patrick McNee.

Ghost Story (1981). Directed by John Irvin. Starring Fred Astaire and Melvyn Douglas.

Haunted (1995). Directed by Lewis Gilbert Starring Aidan Quinn and Kate Beckinsale.

Haunted History. History Channel Home Video. Documentary.

Haunted History of Halloween. History Channel Home Video. Documentary.

Haunted Houses. A & E Home Video. Documentary.

Haunted Places (2001). Documentary by Christopher Lewis.

The Haunting (1999). Directed by Jan de Bont. Starring Liam Neeson and Catherine Zeta-Jones.

Haunting Across America (2001). Documentary hosted by Michael Dorn.

The Haunting of Hell House (1999). Starring Michael York and Claudia Christian.

The Haunting of Julia (1976). Directed by Richard Loncraine. Starring Mia Farrow and Keir Dullea.

Haunting of Louisiana (2000). Documentary. Produced by Barbara Sillery, Lagniappe Media Productions, New Orleans.

The Haunting of Morella (1991). Directed by Jim Wynorski. Starring David McCallum and Nicole Eggert.

The Haunting of Sarah Hardy (1989). Directed by Jerry London. Starring Sela Ward, Michael Woods, and Morgan Fairchild.

The Haunting of Seacliff Inn (1995). Directed by Walter Klenhard. Starring Ally Sheedy and William R. Moses.

Hollywood Ghosts and Gravesites (2003). Documentary.

Lady in White (1988). Directed by Frank LaLoggia. Starring Lukas Haas and Len Cariou.

The Legend of Hell House (1998). Directed by John Hough.

Starring Pamela Franklin, Roddy MacDowell, and Clive Revill.

Living With the Dead (2000). Directed by Stephen Gyllenhaal. Starring Ted Danson and Mary Steenburgen.

The Others (2001). Directed by Alejandro Amenábar. Starring Nicole Kidman and Christopher Eccleston.

Poltergeist (1982). Directed by Tobe Hooper. Starring JoBeth Williams and Craig T. Nelson.

Poltergeist II: The Other Side (1986). Directed by Brian Gibson. Starring JoBeth Williams and Craig T. Nelson.

Restless Spirits (1999). Directed by David Wellington. Starring Lothaire Bluteau, Michel Monty, and Marsha Mason.

Sightings: Heartland Ghost (2002). Directed by Brian Trenchard-Smith. Starring Randy Birch and Beau Bridges.

The Sixth Sense (1999). Directed by M. Night Shyamalan. Starring Bruce Willis and Haley Joel Osment.

The Skeleton Key (2005). Directed by Iain Softley. Starring Kate Hudson and Gena Rowlands.

Thirteen Ghosts (2001). Directed by Steve Beck. Starring Tony Shalhoub.

The Unexplained: Hauntings. A & E Home Video. Documentary.

White Noise (2005). Directed by Geoffrey Sax. Starring Michael Keaton.

The following two movies are not about ghosts, but they are worth watching before visiting New Orleans. They will give you a sneak preview of the some of the scenery and local culture.

The Big Easy (1987). Directed by Jim McBride. Starring Dennis Quaid and Ellen Barkin.

Double Jeopardy (1999). Directed by Bruce Beresford. Starring Tommy Lee Jones and Ashley Judd.

Special Tours and Events

Candlelight Tour of Historic Homes and Landmarks. Every December you can participate in a unique self-guided tour that features the rich history and stunning architecture of New Orleans. The tour is staged in the early evening and includes refreshments. Call 504-522-5730.

Cemetery/Voodoo Tour. With a knowledgeable and entertaining guide, this tour takes you through St. Louis Cemetery Number 1. See fascinating above-ground tombs of famous people. Guides tell humorous and tragic anecdotes, as well as the true histories of some of the notables buried there. The tomb of voodoo priestess Marie Laveau and the *Easy Rider* film site are highlighted. Tour groups meet at Café Beignet, 334-B Royal Street, at 10:00 A.M. and 1:00 P.M. Monday through Saturday and 10:00 A.M. only on Sunday. $15. Call 504-947-2120. E-mail: tourNO@tourneworleans.com.

French Quarter History Tour. Walk the streets of the Vieux Carré with an experienced guide. This 90-minute walking tour takes you from the shores of the Mississippi River to jazz landmarks, film locations, the town's earliest buildings, and Creole courtyards. Tour meets at Café Beignet, 311 Bourbon Street, at 10:30 A.M. daily. $15. Call 504-947-2120. E-mail: tourNO@tourneworleans.com. Web site: www.tourneworleans.com.

Friends of the Cabildo Walking Tour. Cabildo docents guide you through one of the oldest communities in the United States. Tour groups meet at the 1850 House Museum Store on Jackson Square, 523 St. Anne Street, at 10:00 A.M. and 1:30 P.M. Tuesday though Sunday and 1:30 P.M. only on Monday. $10. Call 504-523-3939.

Garden District/Cemetery Tour. This walking tour takes you to the old American sector of New Orleans with a knowledgeable guide. The architecture, oak-lined streets, and social history of the district are contrasted with the French Quarter. You see the homes of writer Anne Rice and Confederate president Jefferson Davis, as well as the famous Lafayette Cemetery Number 1. Tour groups meet at Garden District Book Shop, 2727 Prytania Street, at 11:00 A.M. and 1:45 P.M. daily. $15. Call 504-947-2120. E-mail: tourNO@tourneworleans.com.

Garden District Ghosts and Legends. With a guide, you walk for two hours through the oak-lined streets of the early American district. Featured sites include the famous Castle Inn, the very haunted Magnolia Mansion, and Lafayette Cemetery Number 1. Tour group meets at the Pontchartrain Hotel, 2031 St. Charles Avenue, at 3:00 P.M. daily. $20. Call 504-861-2727. Web site: www.hauntedhistory-tours.com.

Ghost and Vampire Tour. Take a two-hour walk and discover why New Orleans is the most haunted city in America. You visit the sites of numerous tragedies and ghost-generating history. Tour group meets at Royal Blend Coffee House, 621 Royal Street, at 8:15 P.M. $18. Call 504-314-0806.

Ghost Dinner at Chretien Point Plantation. One Friday night each month, Chretien Point Plantation hosts the ghost dinner tour. This includes a wine reception, tour of the 1840s mansion with knowl-edgeable and entertaining guides, and a three-course dinner in the formal dining room. You hear stories about the ghosts that haunt this house and have a chance to experience their ghostly activity. For ghost hunters traveling up the Mississippi River Valley to the central part of Louisiana (ten miles north of Lafayette), this is a rare oppor-tunity to experience antebellum hospitality and history. $49.95. Call 800-880-7050. E-mail: reservations@chretienpoint.com.

Ghosts of New Orleans. This two-hour tour explores the grim and ghastly deeds of the old French Quarter. Theatrical, entertaining, fun, and a bit chilling, this tour takes you to legendary haunted places. Tour groups meet at Rev. Zombie's Voodoo Shop, 723 St. Peter Street, at 2:00 P.M., 4:00 P.M., 6:00 P.M., and 8:00 P.M. daily. $20. Call 504-861-2727.

Haunted French Quarter Walk. Tour America's most haunted city with an experienced guide. This tour takes you to the infamous Lalaurie Mansion, the Sultan's Retreat (a mansion once occupied by a sultan who, along with his entourage, was murdered in the house in 1878), St. Louis Cathedral, the Beauregard-Keyes House, and many other haunted locations. Tour group meets at Bourbon Orleans Hotel, 717 Orleans Street, at 7:30 P.M. daily. $20.00. Contact: 504-947-2120. E-mail: tourNO@tourneworleans.com.

New Orleans Cemetery History Tour. This walking tour takes you to the famous St. Louis Cemetery Number 1 to visit the tomb of voodoo priestess Marie Laveau then on to other famous locations around the French Quarter. You see film locations, the site of the famous brothel the House of the Rising Sun, and the French Mortuary Chapel. Tour groups meet at 625 Royal Street, at 11:00 A.M. and 1:00 P.M. Monday through Saturday and at 10:00 A.M. on Sunday. $15. Call 504-947-2120. Web site: www.tourneworleans.com. Flanagan's Pub, 625 St. Philip Street 504-628-1722

New Orleans Ghost Tour. Your guides on this two-hour walking tour are not only knowledgeable in the history of haunted places, but they are exceptional performers as well. They fascinate participants with ghostly tales and give you an experience that is truly unique. You visit sites of vampire crimes and dark streets where ghostly phenomena are frequently experienced. Tour groups meet at Flanagan's Pub, 625 St. Phillip Street, at 7:00 P.M. and 8:30 P.M. nightly. $19. Call 504-628-1722.

Sacred Roots—A Voodoo Walk. The first hour of this tour takes you on a walk to explore some spiritual aspects and history of the French

Quarter. It includes a visit to the home of voodoo priestess Marie Laveau. The second hour is spent inside Chez Vodun, a voodoo museum and working temple. You witness voodoo blessings and healing rituals. Tour group meets at Flanagan's Pub, 625 St. Phillip Street. $19. Call 504-628-1722. Web site: www.neworleansghosttour.com.

St. Francisville Tours. For ghost hunters traveling north along the Mississippi River Valley to this charming town, St. Francisville Tours offers tours of cemeteries, haunted sites, historical sites, and churches. Call 225-635-6289. Web site: www.stfrancisvilletours.com.

Secret Courtyards of the French Quarter. This two-hour walking tour takes you inside several courtyards. Guides tell stories about the men and women, slaves and free people, who lived or worked in these locations. The tour features the culture and history of old New Orleans interpreted through the writings of a Creole woman, Laura Locoul (1861-1963). Tour groups meet at Le Monde Créole, 624 Royal Street, at 10:30 A.M. and 1:30 P.M. Monday through Saturday and at 10:00 A.M. and 1:30 P.M. on Sunday. $25. Call 504-568-1801. E-mail: creolwrld@bellsouth.net.

Organizations

American Society for Psychical
Research
5 West 73rd Street
New York, NY 10023
212-799-5050

Astrological and Psychical
Society
124 Trefoilo Crescent
Broadfeld, Crawley
West Sussex RH119EZ
England

Berkeley Psychic Institute
2436 Hastings Street
Berkeley, CA 94704
510-548-8020

British Society for Psychical
Research
Eleanor O'Keffe, secretary
49 Marloes Road
London W86LA
England
44-71-937-8984

Center for Scientific Anomalies
Research
P.O. Box 1052
Ann Arbor, MI 48103

Committee for Scientific
Investigations of Claims of the
Paranormal
1203 Kensington Avenue
Buffalo, NY 14215

Division of Parapsychology
Box 152, Medical Center
Charlottesville, VA 22908

Ghost Hunters of the South
(GHOTS)
www.ghots.net

Institute for Parapsychology
Box 6847
College Station
Durham, NC 27708

International Society for
Paranormal Research
4712 Admiralty Way
Marina del Rey, CA 90292

Louisiana Paranormal Research
Society
725 Misty Lane
Lake Charles, LA 70611

New Orleans Paranormal and
Occult Research Society
97 Fontainebleau Dr.
New Orleans, LA 70125-3417
504-861-2727

Office of Paranormal
Investigations
John F. Kennedy University
12 Altarinda Road
Orinda, CA 94563
415-249-9275

Orange County Paranormal
Research Group
www.ocprgroup.com

Parapsychology Foundation
228 E. 71st Street
New York, NY 10021
212-628-1550

Psychical Research Foundation
c/o William Roll
Psychology Department
West Georgia College
Carrolton, GA 30118

San Diego Paranormal Research
Project
www.SDparanormal.com

Saybrook Institute
1772 Vallejo Street
San Francisco, CA 94123

Society for Psychical Research
1 Adam and Eve Mewes
Kensington, W8 6UG
England

Southern California Society for
Psychical Research
269 South Arden Boulevard
Los Angeles, CA 90004

Southern Ghosts
407-616-4697
E-mail:
info@southernghosts.com

Stanford University
Department of Psychology
Jordan Hall, Building 420
Stanford, CA 94305

Appendix F

Internet Resources

www.ghostresearch.com. Web site for information about ghost hunting methods and equipment, as well as ongoing investigations.

www.ghost-stalker.com. Web site of ghost hunter Richard Senate.

www.ghosttowns.com. Informative Web site that gives detailed information about ghost towns in the United States and Canada.

www.ghostweb.com/index.html. Web site of the International Ghost Hunters Society.

www.ghots.net. Web site for Ghost Hunters of the South, an association of researchers and investigators.

www.hauntings.com. Web site for the International Society for Paranormal Research.

www.historichotels.org. Historic hotels of America are detailed here.

www.history.com. Web site of the History Channel.

www.london-ghost-walk.co.uk. Information about tours of London's haunted streets.

www.mindreader.com. A network for students and practitioners of paranormal psychology. It lists events, courses, and certifications.

www.neworleansghosts.com. Features tours of haunted places throughout New Orleans and south Louisiana.

www.nps.gov. Web site of the National Park Service. Locations include many historic sites.

www.psiapplications.com. Psi Applications is dedicated to the investigation and documentation of anomalous events, including the paranormal.

www.southernghosts.com. Highlights tours and events throughout Florida and the Gulf Coast.

www.the-atlantic-paranormal-society.com. Web site of the Atlantic Paranormal Society.

www.technica.com. This is a catalog of electronic detectors and recorders that can be used in ghost hunting.

www.theshadowlands.net/ghost. Ghost stories and information about hauntings in all 50 states.

www.yahoo.com. For maps and driving instructions to a site, click on "Maps." Enter your address or any starting point, then enter the address of the haunted place you wish to visit. Yahoo generates a free map and driving instructions, including estimated driving time and total miles.

Historical Societies and Museums

Historical societies and museums are good places to discover information about old houses and other buildings or places that figure prominently in local history. They often contain records in the form of old newspapers, diaries, and photographs about tragic events such as fires, hangings, train wrecks, and hurricanes that led to loss of life. Old photographs and maps that are not on display for public viewing may be available to serious researchers.

City Archives
New Orleans Public Library
219 Loyola Street
New Orleans, LA 70112
504-596-2610

Confederate Museum
929 Camp Street
New Orleans, LA 70130
540-523-4522

Foundation for Historical
Louisiana
502 North Boulevard
Baton Rouge, LA 70802
225-387-2464

Gretna Historical Society
209 Lafayette Street
Gretna, LA 70053
504-362-3854

Historic Donaldsonville
Museum
318 Mississippi Street
Donaldsonville, LA 70346
225-746-0004

Jackson Barracks Military
Museum
6400 St. Claude Avenue
New Orleans, LA 70117
504-278-8262

Jean Lafitte National Historic
Park and Preserve
365 Canal Street, Suite 3080
Nee Orleans, LA 70130
504-589-3882

Louisiana Genealogical and
Historical Society
P.O. Box 82060
Baton Rouge, LA 70884

Louisiana Historical Society
5801 St. Charles Avenue
New Orleans, LA 70115
504-866-3049

Louisiana Museum of African
American History
1210 Governor Nicholls Street
New Orleans, LA 70116
504-586-1919

Old Arsenal Museum
900 Capitol Lake Drive
Baton Rouge, LA 70802
225-342-0401

Louisiana State Museum
7751 Chartres Street
New Orleans, LA 70116
504-568-6972

Point Coupee Historical Society
500 West Main Street
New Roads, LA 70760
225-638-3800

River Road Historical Society
13034 River Road
Destrehan, LA 70047
985-764-9345

St. James Historical Society
1988 Jefferson Highway
Lutcher, LA 70071
225-869-9752

Ursuline Convent Archives and
Museum
2635 State Street
New Orleans, LA 70118
504-866-1472

Williams Research Center
410 Chartres Street
New Orleans, LA 70130
504-598-7171

Index